Personal Identity in Moral and Legal Reasoning

Richard Prust
St. Andrews University

Jeffery Geller
University of North Carolina, Pembroke

Series in Philosophy of Personalism

Copyright © 2020 Vernon Press, an imprint of Vernon Art and Science Inc, on behalf of the author.

All rights reserved. No part of this publication may be reproduced, stored in a retrieval system, or transmitted in any form or by any means, electronic, mechanical, photocopying, recording, or otherwise, without the prior permission of Vernon Art and Science Inc.

www.vernonpress.com

In the Americas:
Vernon Press
1000 N West Street,
Suite 1200, Wilmington,
Delaware 19801
United States

In the rest of the world:
Vernon Press
C/Sancti Espiritu 17,
Malaga, 29006
Spain

Series in Philosophy of Personalism

ISBN: 978-1-62273-835-9

Also available:

978-1-62273-628-7 [Hardback]; 978-1-62273-747-5 [PDF, E-Book]

Cover designed by Vernon Press. Cover image: http://www.jefferygeller.com/

Product and company names mentioned in this work are the trademarks of their respective owners. While every care has been taken in preparing this work, neither the authors nor Vernon Art and Science Inc. may be held responsible for any loss or damage caused or alleged to be caused directly or indirectly by the information contained in it.

Every effort has been made to trace all copyright holders, but if any have been inadvertently overlooked the publisher will be pleased to include any necessary credits in any subsequent reprint or edition.

Table of Contents

Introduction — *v*

Chapter 1   **Personal Stories** — 1

Chapter 2   **Personal Presence** — 17

Chapter 3   **Personal Rights** — 35

Chapter 4   **Personal Responsibility** — 57

Chapter 5   **Personal Integrity** — 69

Chapter 6   **Prospects for Personhood** — 93

The Axioms of Character Logic — *111*

Bibliography — *113*

Index — *115*

Introduction

The notion that humans have personal identity has fallen on hard times. It has been under attack for the better part of the last century by both British analysts who have analyzed it away and by continental philosophers who have deconstructed it. And so it has come to be that when systematic thinkers set out to understand human behavior in the many ways they do—as economists, neurologists, marketers, and philosophers, to name a few—they shy away from claiming to identify persons. Their reluctance is understandable: given the influence of science and the objectivizing tendency science encourages, it is not surprising that people try to make do with identifying individual somatic actors and discount "personal" identity as the trace of a superannuated conceptual heritage, old and in the way. Psychologists, who should be expected to study persons if anyone does, make do with studying behavior. Even in the humanities, influential voices counsel us to avoid accrediting individually identifiable beings like "the author."

Yet, for some purposes and in some contexts the identification of persons seems intuitive. Each of us knows certain people personally but not others; we extend personal trust to some but not others; we hold some people personally responsible for their action but not others. When we accept someone's personal promise or exchange personal vows, we take ourselves to be interacting with more than a living body. We take ourselves to be interacting with a being who is with us in a way that objects cannot be, someone who is present with us as another person.

For some purposes and in some contexts the identification of persons is socially indispensable. Take the ascribing of personal responsibility. When we find someone morally blameworthy or legally liable for a crime—or, for that matter, morally praiseworthy or legally innocent of a crime—our finding can only count as rational if we depend on some explicable standard for distinguishing actions for which someone bears personal responsibility from those for which he does not. It is certainly not the case that one is personally responsible for all the actions of the body he is; if he were, there would be no distinction between his causal responsibility and his personal responsibility. For example, when someone is driving on a country road and a deer springs, seemingly out of nowhere, into the car's path, the driver, though causally implicated, would not be held personally responsible for the deer's injury.

One might think that what gets the driver off the hook is that he did not intend to hit the deer. But while intending to do something is usually indicative of personal responsibility, there are cases in which we blame people for harm they didn't intend. For example, someone whose cell phone rings during the performance of a string quartet bears personal responsibility for having let that happen. There are also cases in which someone intends an action but bears no personal responsibility for it: a two-year-old in some primitive sense intended to scribble on the wall but we do not blame him personally for his vandalism.

What we propose to do in this book is to uncover the criterion we use in practice to ascribe moral and legal rights and responsibilities. We are going to argue that for those purposes—which we will sometimes lump together as "forensic" purposes—supplying a clear distinction between actions for which someone bears personal responsibility and those for which he does not is tantamount to providing an account of his personal identity.

We are aware that setting off to account for personal identity, particularly to account for the criterion of personal identity governing moral and legal reasoning, will strike many philosophers as quixotic. We've already admitted that Anglophone analysts have concluded from various thought experiments—brain transplants, implants, and teleports—that it is impossible to provide a coherent account of individual personal identity that is useful in moral and legal decision-making, and that, transfixed by the contingency of meaning, many continental philosophers have given up on identity of any sort.

But our approach to the issue of personal identity will proceed along an entirely different course. We will look for clues in how people actually reason when they ascribe an action to a person. Instead of writing off popular patterns of reasoning as "folk psychology" we will show that there are coherent patterns in the ways we typically connect the character of somebody's action and his identity as the person acting. We will argue for the following:

1. In ordinary interactions we identify somebody personally as the present character of his resolve. "Resolve" will be a crucial term in our account of identity, so what we mean by "the present character of his resolve" will require some unpacking, to be sure. While we will be trying to give systematic rigor to that term, we will not be departing from ordinary usage. We say, for instance, of someone highly resolved to win the country club tennis championship that she is "putting a lot of herself" into winning, meaning that she is coordinating a good deal of her active life in that pursuit. So we seem intuitively grounded when we think of someone's resolve as his determination to accomplish something in coordination with other elements of his intentional life. The first chapter will demonstrate how this common sense understanding of resolve can be spelled out in terms of a for-

mal feature that characterizations of action bear when they count as resolute.

2. This formal feature—marking some actions as resolved and others as not resolved—is what governs us when we ascribe moral or legal responsibility. In other words, identifying somebody personally in terms of the character of his resolve determines what moral and legal judgments it is reasonable to make about him and his action.

3. By codifying the rules we follow when drawing inferences about someone's resolve—rules that jointly constitute what we will call character logic—we can shed light on some of the perennial issues that arise in connection with ascribing personal rights and responsibilities.

Let us hasten to assure readers that discerning the patterns of inference that comprise character logic will not require mastery of some new notational scheme or challenge us with anything esoteric. We need only make ourselves mindful of some of the general features of claims about what people do, claims like, "Babe Ruth hit 60 home runs in 1927," "William Howard Taft took office in 1909," "Bonnie runs the clothing department at Wal-Mart," "Tesla produces electric cars," and "tigers eat meat." We will represent such claims as having an 'A did C' form. That is, they are all claims that 'a certain agent A did (does, will do) an action of a certain character C.' We will call them "character claims." Character logic is simply the logic we use to draw inferences from character claims. This will become clearer when we consider examples.

The best way to see what is distinct about character claims is to hold them up against the kind of claims Aristotle operated with in his logic of categories. Aristotle invited us to think of truth claims as claims about how classes or categories are related. If, along life's way, you took a course in category logic you may recall the four ways he showed us in which statements can relate the categories they contain: All S is P, No S is P, Some S is P, and Some S is not P. These standard form category claims each have a subject (S) term and a predicate (P) term. Every S or P term denotes a class or category. Accordingly, any category claim about S and P can be read as a claim about the inclusion or exclusion of the members of one class by the other. For example, to say that all rabbits are mammals is to say that every member of the rabbit class is a member of the mammal class; to say that no Red Sox fans are Yankee fans is to say that all Red Sox fans are excluded from the class of Yankee fans and vice versa.

Though Aristotle believed there are different kinds of knowledge, each with its own virtue and kind of wisdom, he held that category logic governs all rational thought. Practical virtue and theoretical virtue, according to him, both require the formulation of rational arguments, the simplest and most helpful of which is the syllogism. His emphasis on syllogistic logic—the logic of inference about class membership—prevented him from appreciating that a different form of logic is necessary to account for the emergence of the subjects we call persons.

This is what limits us when we use category logic to reason about what people do: it requires us to assume that what we are calling character claims can be rendered successfully, albeit awkwardly, in one of the standard forms truth claims take. It means that claims ascribing a character of action C to an agent A can be rendered as claims predicating a category of action P to a subject S. While this is unobjectionable in many cases, there are exceptions, and it is the exceptions that make reasoning with character claims distinctive and, we will argue, indispensable in forensic contexts.

Imagine this little vignette: two people hear that "Kay bought a used car." The Aristotelian assumption would be that both of them heard a claim that was, for formal purposes, that "All people identical to Kay are (members of the category of) people who bought a used car." But now imagine that the two people, Jay and Bea, differ in how well they know Kay. Bea knows Kay as a friend, let us say, while Jay has yet to meet her. Since the only thing Jay knows about Kay is that she bought a used car, characterizing Kay's action by putting her in the category of used car buyers completely captures what he understands of her action. But not so for Bea. To her, "Kay bought a used car" discloses a far richer and more complex truth. She knows that Kay recently lost her house in a foreclosure and that she has had to sell her Lexus. And Bea knows that the way Kay's divorce was finalized means that she now has to struggle to find a new financial equilibrium and that buying a used car was a telling step in her scaling back for the sake of a better fresh start.

What makes Bea's awareness of Kay different from Jay's involves Bea's acquaintance with some of the other strands of Kay's intentional life into which her car purchase is woven. Kay (to Bea) presents herself (in the act of buying the car) as a thread in a tapestry of active significance rather than just a discrete act. Buying that car bears more than its category meaning; it reveals her laudable pluck.

The richness of character that Bea sees in Kay's action (but Jay does not) is our starting point in this account of personal identity. We are going to look for certain features—formal features, as we will explain below—the character of Kay's action had for Bea that it did not have for Jay. Discerning that distinctiveness in Bea's grasp of Kay's action will enable us to see how the character of Kay's action identifies her (for Bea) personally.

Introduction ix

We have been referring to the "form" ('A does C') our characterization of somebody's action takes. That may strike you as a puzzling reference, particularly since we are suggesting that we cannot simply identify actions by categories when we reason in moral and legal contexts. So let us provide a few examples of what we mean by formal features. First, it is a formal feature of characterizations of actions that they are embedded in character claims, claims that have the form of an ascription of an action to an agent. In other words, we do not characterize action without imputing it to an agent; we do not claim that 'C' but that 'A did C.' What makes this crucial to recognize is that it presents us with a clear contrast, as we will demonstrate, between character logic and category logic. Though it may seem that our focus on the *formal* features of character claims introduces an unnecessary complication, the contrast between category logic and character logic comes through most clearly when we juxtapose the form of character claims ('A does C') to the form of categorical propositions (any one of Aristotle's four proposition types from 'All S is P' to 'Some S is not P'). We must ask therefore a certain degree of indulgence on the part of readers who are unfamiliar with Aristotelian category logic or uncomfortable with symbolic notation. The formal analysis, which might seem forbidding at the beginning, will become easier as we proceed.

If we use category logic in ascribing C to A, we understand A to be a subject term to which we predicate an action categorized as C. When we identify A as a member of a category, we assume that A has its own independent meaning (expressed in terms of membership in a class) apart from C. This generates the problem of identifying the agent of an action apart from any particular action we ascribe to him, a feat—and here we agree with the consensus—that is impossible to pull off in a forensically useful way.

Our approach, by contrast, recognizes that when a character claim identifies somebody personally (such as "Kay bought a used car" did for Bea) the identity of the agent can be read out of the character of the action ascribed. We are going to show that A—when A names a person—has no meaning apart from C—when C has the kind of richness it had for Bea. We are going to show that the richness of C bestows a character identity upon A and gives A the only personal identity he has. In contrast to category logic, which presupposes that A and C are semantically independent, character logic presupposes that A and C are mutually semantically dependent. We will have more to say about this later in the introduction.

Character claims have other formal features that are going to prove crucial for our account. In standard cases the actions they characterize play themselves out over a stretch of time: they each have an inception and a completion, even if we can fix those limits only vaguely. Another distinctive formal feature is that we can classify any act we characterize as either socially interactive or not. Still another is that an act C bears a positive or negative value for its agent. We will explore the implications of each of these features of character claims as they bear on the question of identity.

By clarifying these features of our characterizations of action and the character claims in which they are lodged, the distinctive features of character logic become apparent. Moreover, the formal features of character claims will be found to determine the standards we depend on when ascribing personal rights and responsibilities.

We have already anticipated one of our core observations: the person-identifying feature of characterizations of action is what we call "resolve." Thinking of resolve this way—as a form somebody's character of action can take—marks a departure from the usual approach of looking for factors independent of an action's character that determine it as resolute, factors like the strong motive force behind it or its high rank among intentional priorities. In the first chapter, our task will be to discern the form a characterization of action has to have if it is to count as resolved. That form can be discerned by describing the kind of imaginative feat it takes to project resolute action. It turns out that resolving to do something involves a feat formally akin to telling a conventional story.

After disclosing the formal similarities, we will also note two telling differences. Having compared and contrasted personal resolve with conventional narrative resolve, we will be able to distinguish a form of narration that may reasonably be called "telling a personal story." This form of storytelling is personal in that it determines a character of resolve and thereby determines someone's personal identity. The upshot of this analysis will be that we treat a person reasonably—for moral and legal purposes—when we treat him as the resolve he presently projects in his personal story.

We are going to see that thinking of a person as the character of his resolve ascribes to him a body of movement that reaches beyond his own intentional life. It reaches into the lives of those he interacts with by inflecting the character of their actions as well as accomplishments by others in the future. An account of all three of these registers is required to represent the being of a person since they all represent ranges of movement determined in character by the character of his resolve.

The second chapter explores the distinctive presence persons have with one another interactively. Persons can be present in ways entities cannot. While that seems obvious in everyday encounters, it has proved puzzling and elusive for those who identify actions with categories. We can make better sense of personal presence if we recognize the distinctive temporal logic governing character claims. One way to focus on this distinctiveness is to compare our use of the word "moment" when we talk about actions with our use of it when we talk about natural events. Whereas a moment of action, as mentioned above, spans the time between its inception and its completion, events mark outcomes. Since e-vents, understood etymologically, are out-comes of causal antecedents, this tends to situate them at points in time. Recognizing this distinction allows us to make sense of our perception that some achievements are of greater moment than others.

Applying a temporal logic of action to reasoning about resolved intentional lives also gives us a basis for making sense of personal presence. Persons are variably present according to the moments of action we see resolved in their lives. They have temporal volume. By clarifying the notion of the volumetric presence of a person, we will be able to understand some important features of how a person's resolve governs our forensic reasoning about him.

Chapter three begins our account of how our regard for persons as characters of resolve justifies many of the moral and legal inferences we intuitively draw. (Though many people use the word "intuition" to dodge an appeal to reason, in this account intuitions can be justified as reasonable. What we are calling an intuition is nothing more mysterious than the tug of character logic as it tries to assert its legitimate governance over our inferences in such matters.) We turn first to the issue of rights. There is, we will argue, a range of rights intrinsic to being a present character of personal resolve. We will have seen in chapter 1 that people resolve their intentions so as to enhance their success as intentional beings. That being the case, to be resolved is to intend the greatest satisfaction of one's intentional life. We will see that the personal right to optimize one's resolve can be asserted in two ways, as the positive right to initiate any interaction that promises to actualize one more momentously and as the negative right to withdraw from any interaction that promises to limit one's self-actualization. I have a positive right to engage you interactively whenever doing so promises to actualize me most. You have the negative right to turn me down when the interaction is not similarly promising for you or, alternatively, to break it off when it no longer holds that promise. Instead of calling these turn-down rights "negative," we are going to call them "absolute," not only because "absolve" is implicit in that word but because "absolute" reflects the precedence the rights they name have over positive rights.

We will show how this account of positive and absolute rights sheds light on a wide variety of thorny issues arising among people who discuss rights. To name a few: it gives some purchase on the elusive notion of universal rights if we think of them as "personal rights" rather than "human rights." It makes clearer sense of the scope of damages we find reasonable to assess by seeing how it correlates with the loss of active moment in the life of the plaintiff. It shows us how a contract can be construed as a personal promise, how it makes sense to outlaw certain advertising as deceptive, how it makes sense to determine what acts of law-breaking should be respected as civil disobedience, and even how it determines grounds for divorce that respect the persons concerned.

Lest you think, given the brevity of this book, that we are promising too much, let us hasten to emphasize the modesty of what we hope to achieve. To accomplish our task, we need only highlight some of the inferential moves people actually make in determining when someone has a right to do something and to show that those moves are underwritten by an awareness of the inherent positive and absolute right to be a person, an awareness that allows us to solve some of the puzzles that stymie us when category logic governs the discussion.

Chapter four explores the basis we have for holding somebody personally responsible for his action, both in judging that he is responsible and, if he is, how blameworthy (or praiseworthy) he is. It argues that A is personally responsible for all and only the actions A does resolutely. The equivalence between the actions that are elements in A's resolve and the action for which he bears personal responsibility is guaranteed by the semantic interdependence of A and C we noted earlier: when we ascribe personal responsibility not only is the A term implicit in the C term but the A term and the C term are mutually implied. C, understood in the context of A's resolve, implies A. And A, understood as a character of resolve, has C as an integral part.

This logical peculiarity—the mutual implication of A and C that is implicit in character claims that identify persons—also turns out to determine how blameworthy or praiseworthy A is for C. Making that assessment, we will see, is always a matter of assessing the momentary damage or satisfaction brought about by A in doing C and the volume of A's personal presence in that moment.

We will survey the kinds and degrees of personal responsibility one might incur under the various formal relations A and C can have in ascriptions of responsibility: 1) A's action C can be resolved in a personal story fully comprehensive of her intentional life (we will be using feminine pronouns gender-inclusively but distinctively to designate persons—if such there be—who are fully integrated in their intentional being): we would hold such a person fully responsible for C. 2) A's action C can be resolved in a personal story that is only partially comprehensive of A's intentional life: we would hold such a person responsible for C but recognize his responsibility as diminished. 3) A's action C can be irresolute: we judge that such a person acted irresponsibly in doing C. 4) A can be a character of resolve no longer narratively coherent with

C: we would rightly forgive such a person. 5) A can be judged to have acted while not yet being or no longer being a character of resolve: we would not hold such an agent personally responsible for C even in a diminished way.

In chapter five we take up an apparent anomaly that will have emerged when we examined the practice of person-respecting societies in preventing people from exploiting one another or in punishing them when they do. It would confound our account if an offender could reasonably claim that exploiting others is what actualizes him best. If he could plausibly make that claim, we could not justify stopping him from acting that way, much less imprisoning him. To rebut this objection, we must show that it is reasonable to believe in the inconceivability of actualizing oneself best by exploiting others. Nothing we will have found up to this point gives us grounds for believing that. Nothing we will have found up to this point supports the thesis that someone can only be most fully actualized living in harmony with others.

We can call this belief—that actualizing oneself best can only be achieved in harmony with the interests of others—a belief in moral integrity. The "integrity" part of this belief does not pose a problem. It is easy to see from a practical standpoint that the better someone resolves or integrates his life, the more of what he intends is likely to be accomplished. But it is quite another matter to say that he has the best prospect for integration when he is in harmony with the intentional lives of those he interacts with. The question we have to answer is, why should anyone believe that the quest to actualize oneself most momentously is also a moral undertaking?

To answer this question, we need to look back into the early history of the notion of a person as an individual being. The narrative imagination it takes to identify individual persons was not available early in the history of our species. Neither then was the possibility of moral integrity, which, if it exists, must characterize individuals. That kind of identity, we will argue, first came to be fixed as a narrative possibility in the sacred stories told by Western monotheists.

Needless to say, today that provenance tends to make people suspicious. But what these early monotheists were required to believe in order to support their belief in moral integrity is not the stumbling block it is widely taken to be. Removing that block will involve analyzing ethical monotheism into the three formal character claims it comprises. We are going to see that all of them are rational claims in the sense that they are subject to confirmation or disconfirmation on the basis of evidence from people's ordinary experience.

While chapter 5 tries to show how the notion of moral integrity got started and what evidence is relevant to judging whether it is actually a human possibility, chapter 6 explains why the question of moral integrity matters. It argues that persons identified in the absence of grounds for affirming the possibility of their moral integrity are systematically diminished in all three dimensions of their personal being: by the compromised coherence of their individual intentional lives, by the diminished scope of their communal possibilities, and by the foreshortened historical importance of what they do.

The prospects for sustaining person-respecting societies, we will argue, depend on whether we can rationally affirm the prospect of moral integrity. If our account of personhood and moral integrity is cogent, the resulting understanding of the personal sustains and broadens those prospects.

A preliminary note is in order about the way we will be using ordinary language in our attempt to recover the person as a subject of rational discourse. Our use of certain words (for example, "moment," "intention," "resolve") may already have struck you as eccentric. Our claim is that identifying persons requires us to hear in the uses of some common terms the meanings they bore before the nearly exclusive dominance of category logic. The modern uses of these words have often occluded their older meanings, meanings that reflect their original character logical governance. If we listen for that etymologically prior use, we can usually hear a clue about how the terms function to inform our intuitions. We have already noticed how a moment of action differs from the moment of an event. When we remind ourselves of the active meaning of "moment", the word becomes transparent to "momentum," the "movement" that determines it. Or take the word, "satisfying." If it seems odd to hear talk about someone satisfying his intentions, that is because we usually think of satisfaction in causal terms, like satisfying an itch by scratching it or satisfying a craving for cashews by eating a handful. But to satisfy originally meant to make enough, so to satisfy an intention is to make enough movement to accomplish it. Or take the word "importance." An act's importance is not the same as an event's importance. The latter refers to consequences while the former refers to the weight of active moment: how much active moment does the meaning of my act carry into my moment of resolve?

To help avoid confusion, you occasionally may want to consult the axioms of character logic we will be exploring; they are compiled at the end of the book.

Chapter 1

Personal Stories

Trying to make sense of personal identity has been a perennial concern of philosophers through much of the Christian era. During that long stretch of time, much of which was dominated by Aristotelian category logic, the challenge was taken to be one of designating what predicate term accurately distinguishes "person" from everything else. For Boethius a person is an individual substance of a rational nature[1], for Locke a thinking intelligent being that has reason and reflection and can consider itself as itself.[2] For P. F. Strawson a person is an individual with both states of consciousness and corporeal characteristics[3], for Harry Frankfurt, someone with second order desires[4], for Lynne Rudder Baker, someone with a continuing first-person perspective.[5]

In that tradition it was assumed that the individual subjects we were trying to identify were "substantial." But the near abandonment of substance metaphysics has collapsed that consensus in our time with the result that identifying "persons" is seen as problematic. Whereas Boethius in the sixth century thought he could reasonably assume that a person, whatever else he was, was a substance (defined by its rationality), by the eighteenth century that confidence was wearing thin. For Locke, one critic notes, "personhood…is more like *being magnetized* than like *being iron or being a saucepan.*"[6] Eventually philosophical accounts came to rely on bare logical placeholders, like Strawson's "individual" or Frankfurt's and Baker's "someone." But this tactic purports to predicate a category without identifying the subject of which it is predicated. It is as though the appropriate predicate could, as it did for An-

---

[1] Boethius, "A Treatise Against Eutyches and Nestorius," *The Theological Treatises*, translated by H. F. Stewart London: Heinemann (1998), p. 85.
[2] John Locke, An Essay Concerning Human Understanding (London: J. M. Dent; NY: Dutton, 1961), p. 280.
[3] Peter Strawson, Peter, *Individuals* (London: Methuen, 1959), p. 104.
[4] Harry Frankfurt, Harry, "Freedom of the Will and the Concept of a Person," in *Free Will*. Gary Watson, ed. (Oxford: Oxford University Press, 1982), pp. 81-95.
[5] Lynne Rudder Baker, Lynne Rudder, *Persons and Bodies: A Constitution View.* (Cambridge University Press, 2000).
[6] Teichman, Jenny, "The Definition of a Person," *Philosophy* LX (1985), p. 180.

selm in his ontological argument for God's existence, define an entity into being.

In our own time we seem to have lost any generally accepted philosophical basis for believing in an identifiable personal self. Analytic philosophers, influenced by Hume's contention that the self is nothing more than a bundle of perceptions, find a lack of any intrinsic mutual belongingness among the whole batch of somebody's experiences (perceptions, memories, active awareness, anticipation, ruminations, dreams, etc.). Continental thinkers, expelled from Eden by the demons of contingency, insist that the myriad narrative sources for the character of somebody's action make it naïve to claim that he bears narrative individuality. To affirm the exclusive legitimacy of any one narrative, according to Jean-François Lyotard, is an exercise in repression. The analyst Jacques Lacan maintained that the unified self is an imaginary construct, a mere illusion. Led by Jacques Derrida, others maintain that wisdom requires that we deconstruct "identities" and allow ourselves to frolic in fragmentation, enjoying all the masks, de-centered constructs, and fleeting roles to which we are subject.

The jaws of reduction and deconstruction having all but chewed up the self where personhood was once thought to dwell, there is no point in trying to salvage any of it, much less rebuild on the same foundation. To rehouse personal identity, our edifice will have to arise in another discursive neighborhood, one governed by character logic instead of category logic. Be assured that we are already very much at home in this neighborhood; we know its inferential byways by heart. After all, characterizing actions is something we have been doing since we learned to talk.

How do we know that this is the right neighborhood for our building project? Because the most obvious and natural way to tell someone who a person is is to characterize his actions. Who's Toni? She works with Pete's mother and hangs out with Penny. Who's Penny? She's the vamp who seduced Uncle Don. But while we typically answer "who" questions with character claims, you will recall that understanding a character claim does not necessarily identify who the agent is. The claim has to be heard in a certain context. Only Bea comprehended who Kay was (in "Kay bought a used car") because only she knew Kay as a character of resolve; while she fathomed Kay's character in at least some of its rich particularity, Jay could only identify Kay as somebody who had bought a used car.

It makes sense then to reframe the identity question this way: what has to be true of a characterization of action (C) in an 'A did C' claim for C to identify A as a person? While Aristotle contended that the truth of any claim is a matter of how its categories are related (inclusively or exclusively, particularly or universally), our account contends that the truth of any person-identifying character claim is a matter of how the personal knowledge we have of A is related to the characterization C. While Aristotle's logic can relate the subject and predicate terms only if they both represent categories, our account can relate the A and C terms because they both represent characters of action.

So then, what form would C have to take in order to identify A's personal character?

The C in 'A did C' claims

Let us go back again to the observation we made earlier about the richness of character Bea heard in the news of Kay's purchase. We suggested that Jay's understanding of what Kay did was distinct from Bea's in that his could (while hers could not) be reduced without residue to a category claim. All he knew of Kay was that (C) she bought a used car. Aristotelian category logic would work perfectly well in any inference he might draw. In contrast, what Bea heard was by no means exhausted by a claim about her membership in the class of people who bought a used car.

We mentioned earlier that it is going to prove crucial in our account to acknowledge the temporal logic of character claims. Only by keeping this in mind will we be able to appreciate the form a character of action has to take to manifest resolve. Consider, for example, the temporal frames Kay's action had for Bea and Jay. For Jay, what Kay did was at a particular time on the morning of June 12. But for Bea, because she sees buying the car as a move in restoring Kay's financial equilibrium, C has for her the character of a temporally broader undertaking. What she was doing in buying the car was not fully executed in the moment of signing the purchase contract. Her on-going accomplishment of restoring financial equilibrium will take more moves over more time.

It is worth noting how the broader temporal moment implicit (for Bea) in Kay's action gets obscured by the assumption that actions are best understood as *out-comes* of causal antecedents, *e-vents*. Thinking of an action as an outcome tends to register its time-frame on the chronological continuum at the point at which the effect of its causal antecedents occurs. Accordingly, philosophers of action who adopt causal accounts of action tend to adopt the temporal logic appropriate to reasoning about events. Their paradigms of intentional behavior represent actions that are accomplished in one move, like flipping a switch with the intention of turning on the light,[7] raising one's

---

[7] Davidson, Donald (1980) *Essays on Actions and Events*. Oxford: Oxford University Press, p. 4.

arm with the intention of signaling a turn,[8] or shooting a man with the intention of killing him.[9] This set them up to ignore the more comprehensive accomplishments in the context of which people normally understand what they are doing, the very kind of undertakings that Bea considered when she grasped the personal meaning of Kay's purchase.

An action, unlike an event, represents a body of movement, all the movement used in accomplishing it. Because movements are momentary, in the sense of that word specified earlier, actions are variable in their temporal thickness. This variability in the moments of our action, particularly of our personal action, will be of central concern in the next chapter. But in this chapter we can begin to unpack it by considering the different ways our actions can be said to relate to one another in time. They can come one after another (Kay ate a simple breakfast and then took the bus to the used car lot), they can be contemporaneous (All the while Kay was eating breakfast she was talking to her mother on the phone), and they can also be simultaneous (Jay came to regret his decision just as he clicked on the "buy" button). But there is one more way they can be related, one especially significant for our purposes. Actions can be temporally nested in each other.

"Look, there's Dee backing out of her garage. She's driving to work." Both character claims about what Dee is presently doing are true. But we would miss something crucial about their relationship—that the first moves the second toward completion—if we saw them as simultaneous. 'Backing out of her garage' is a move Dee is making in 'driving to work.' This possibility for ordering our character claims—one as a move in the other's accomplishment—determines three rules of inference about action, rules we will depend on in the account ahead:

1. The character of each nested action is implicit in the other. Driving to work is implicit in what backing out meant to Dee and backing out is part of what driving to work meant to her.

2. The moment of each is understood as included in the other. The moment of backing out is present in the thick moment of driving to work. Moreover, the thick moment of driving to work is present in the moment of backing out. The former inclusion, because of the obvious chronological embeddedness, may seem more obvious than the latter. The latter inclusion—the inclusion of the longer chronological expanse in the shorter—only becomes apparent on those special occasions when a simple moment of movement – like slip-

---

[8] Melden, A. I. (1961), *Free Action*. London: Routledge and Kegan Paul, p. 19.
[9] Swinburne, R. (1986), *The Evolution of the Soul*. Oxford: Clarendon Press, p. 87.

ping a wedding ring on somebody's finger – is understood to bear far greater moment.
3. The actual being of each is included in the other. In the act of backing out Dee actually was driving to work and in the act of driving to work she actually backed out.

If we keep in mind these three rules governing our reasoning about actions, we can begin to make sense of the thickness of personal significance only Bea could appreciate in Kay's act. But before we can do that we need to make a first pass at describing features of character claims as they pertain to the A term.

The A in 'A did C' claims

We announced in the Introduction that the formal peculiarity about the identity of A in 'A did C' claims (when A identifies a person) is that A cannot be identified apart from C. Let us try to make that point clearer by contrasting it with A as it is used in impersonal ascriptions. When a referee calls a foul on #21 he does so impersonally: it is enough that he identifies the agent as somebody wearing #21 on his jersey. In that case, player #21's agency is predetermined in its scope so that the referee knows full well what makes a foul #21's foul. This is true even when A incorporates a large number of individual somebodies. For example, when the Vice President for Public Relations says, "We of the Acme Corporation are achieving monumental synergies with the merger we are announcing today," the range of actions properly ascribable to "we of the Acme Corporation" includes those of many people—employees, consultants, lawyers and others—yet it includes only *some* of their actions. (Not even the most avid corporate career climber identifies with his job entirely.) And while the range of action for a committee, corporation or nation is often the subject of litigation, that litigation is only possible because there is a more or less articulated determination of that range in the form of statutes and common law traditions as well as other legal, customary, and contractual boundaries. If Acme were to be challenged in court, accepted rules, laws, and practices could be relied upon to determine, say, whether some employee's offense was his responsibility or that of the corporation.

To make the case that personal ascriptions are different—in that in person-identifying 'A did C' claims A does *not* have a prescribed identity—we must account for just how C determines A's scope as an agent. Ascriptions about A's moral or legal responsibility for C are particularly prominent in forensic discussions, but we should keep in mind that there is a scope of personal agency identified in any person-identifying 'A did C' claim, not only in ascriptions that hold A personally responsible for C but in those that praise A's personal integrity in doing C or in which A makes a personal vow to C. In all of these ascriptions, we want to argue, the scope of A's movement (for which he bears personally responsibility, in which he bears personal integrity, or in whose name he plights his troth) can be appropriately determined by a character-rich reading of C. Agent A in other words emerges as identifiable because C bears in its character, richly understood, *who* A is. Who A is, in turn, is determined in the scope of action personally ascribable to him.

To set ourselves up to see how C, richly understood, identifies A (when 'A did C' ascribes to A personally) we should perhaps remind ourselves what makes us perceive an element of behavior as an action in the first place. Action, we agree, is intentional behavior. That is, if C is A's action and not just his unintentional behavior—like blushing at a compliment or starting when a gun discharges—we presume that A's movement intends C through the course of C's accomplishment. Action is not just bodily movements; it is movements bearing on a characterizable achievement. When Grandma cries, "Look, she's crawling to me!" it is of course Grandma doing the characterizing. Yet she and we assume that there is an analog in baby's awareness, that some infantile intention is being sustained in her movement under some figure in her active awareness. That is why we say of anybody who intends to do something that he "means" to do it and of anybody who means to do something that he intends it. So we will stipulate that if A did C, even if C was a very primitive act, A meant to do C, which is to say, A was aware of moving in some fashion we characterize as C.

Might we then fix the range of somebody's intentional behavior as the range of his personal responsibility? Though that would be conceptually elegant, it would not exactly square with how we assign personal responsibility. If I run across your newly seeded lawn, a Doberman pincher lunging at my heels, in some sense I must have it in mind to cut across your lawn and *mean* to do so. But even though my dash counts as intentional, I trust you would not hold my trespass against me ... the negligent owner of the Doberman perhaps, not me.

We have of course already tipped our hand as to the type of intentional behavior that, in our view, discloses the logic of our forensic judgments. We will defend the view that moral and legal reasoning recognizes a person as the present character of his resolve. That makes our challenge one of describing formally what it means for some action C or some person A to be resolute or resolved. What is it about the character of a person's intention that qualifies it as resolute? Once we understand the distinctive form an action's character must have if it is to count as resolved we will be in a position to tell whether the sphere of personal responsibility, so determined, governs our moral and legal reasoning in practice. Accordingly, the remainder of this chapter explores what it means for an action to be resolved.

We said earlier that the richer meaning Bea saw in Kay's car purchase had to do with how Bea saw the purchase fitting into Kay's life as a whole. That is what made her understanding of the car purchase different from Jay's: her tacit awareness of other of Kay's intentions in the context of which her purchase had its richer significance. But simply being aware of some broader range of Kay's intentions would not necessarily constitute an awareness of Kay as a person. To have a personal awareness of Kay, Bea had to be aware of how Kay was coordinating her life and how her purchase fit into that coordination. She was not merely buying a used car. In so doing she was scaling back her standard of living, modifying her life in order to recover financially from her divorce and transitioning to a new chapter of her life. Buying the car played into a more comprehensive strategy for bringing her intentional life into a new equilibrium, one that promised to serve her interests better, and it was in that coordination that Bea found Kay the person, there in the context of mutual accommodations wherein her acts had a joint significance. My act of dashing across your newly seeded lawn had no such context.

So then, how do we become aware of an agent's personal identity in the way we see him coordinating his life? What form must the comprehensive meaning of his actions take in order to identify him as a person?

Resolve as the realm of the personal

What we are after here is a formal definition of personal resolve that enables us to understand how it can be identified by the character of what someone does. So far, all we have said about someone's intentional coordination is that it involves imaginatively projecting a way to coordinate multiple intentions by way of providing for their mutual accommodation. So the question now is, can somebody's intentional coordination bear a single identity? How can a multi-intentioned actor have a singular character?

Consider first how we characterize the coordination of action at a more basic level. Suppose you spot a stranger taking your luggage off the airport carousel. It dawns on you: "Hey, that's my suitcase! He's taking my suitcase!" At that instant, "taking my suitcase" is the only characterization you can reasonably make of what this person is doing. You know that there is something wrong or mistaken in what he is doing, but you are not yet in a position to make moral or legal sense of it. He might have grabbed it by mistake, but he might be stealing it. No telling yet, not before you can discover something about the active context of his deed. If you then spotted the same stranger hurrying back from the parking deck, your suitcase in tow, straining toward the lost luggage office and blushing with chagrin, you'd shrug him off as some irresponsible oaf, careless but not criminal. But if you chased after him just in time to see him duck behind a car rental counter and cut off your luggage tags, you would conclude he was a thief.

Alright, the stranger was a thief, and you were right to conclude that from what you saw in the chase. Now the police arrive and ask you what makes you so sure the stranger was stealing the suitcase. The most likely way you would answer would be to tell a little story: "I chased him down to the opposite end of the baggage claim area where I saw him duck behind Kwicky's Karental Kounter and clip the tags off my suitcase. Officer, this guy obviously meant to steal my luggage."

You could tell this little story with a very short series of character claims. But presumably the police would hear your story not just as a series of claims but as a series of claims that got resolved in their meaning by your characterization, "stole my luggage." That characterization resolves the narrative in the sense that it allows us to comprehend the series under a singular characterization, much as the character of Dee's "backing out of the garage" resolved itself along with other elements of her action in "driving to work."

What we want to show now is that a narrative of sorts is called for to represent somebody's overall resolve, that is, the coordination by virtue of which he emerges as an individual. But here we have to tread carefully. The character of somebody's personal resolve can indeed be said to have the form of a story, and we will be drawing on the analogies between how persons are resolved and how narratives are resolved. But we will be misled if we overlook the differences between them. Our approach to understanding the form of personal resolve will be to compare it to and contrast it with the form of resolution a conventional storyteller aims at. If we keep both the analogies and the dis-analogies in mind, our contention is that we can represent the distinctive form of storytelling we use to identify present characters of resolve.

Among the analogies between a conventional narrative's resolution and somebody's imaginative projection of resolve there are four in particular we will depend on: (1) Both narrative and personal resolve have the significant form of a course of action projected imaginatively to accomplish a set of intentional undertakings. (2) In both narrative and personal resolve the course projected is more or less inclusive of a determined range of intentional life to which it is accountable. (3) Both projections purport to be optimally comprehensive of that range. And (4) we make rational judgments about the relative success of both a conventional narrative's resolution and an individual's imaginative projection of resolve. We will consider these analogies in turn.

(1) Both personal and narrative resolve are imaginative projections that chart a course of action.

In the case of conventional narratives the imaginative projection is a plotline in which all the subplots are woven together. That makes the way a conventional story's resolution completes the meaning of the episodes more complex than how "stole my suitcase" completed the meaning of the narrative you used to justify your characterization of the stranger's dastardly act. Both, however, represent a characterization that resolves its episodes and adds richness to the meaning of each.

Analogously, personal resolve takes the form of an imaginative projection that is meant to coordinate a set of elements, in this case the various commitments, involvements, appointments, and relationships that configure someone's on-going pursuits. To perceive his action as resolved is to perceive it as accommodating of and accommodated by other of his intentional pursuits.

To make this analogy clearer, imagine reading in an op-ed piece that your senator has resolved to seek the nomination of her party as candidate for President. This news surprises you, and you wonder whether there is anything to it. What might convince you one way or the other? Suppose you had insider contacts who told you she'd begun talking to rich people about campaign funds and huddling with consultants about what issues to campaign on, that she had begun preparing her family for the ordeal, and that she is staffing ground operations in several states. The columnist, you would conclude, is probably right. But, on the other hand, if you couldn't discover her making any such moves in preparation for a run you'd have to suspect that the writer was rumor-mongering.

(2) In both narrative and personal resolve the course projected is more or less inclusive of a determined range of intentional life to which it is accountable.

In a conventional narrative like a novel, a play, or a movie script, what gets resolved ideally is the whole of the related action. A critic might point to ingenious ways the elements (editing, character chemistry, plot, script, and lighting) worked together or failed to work together. He would hold the *auteur* accountable for using every scene and device to tell the story, the novelist every episode, the playwright every line, the director every angle, prop and block. And it would be against that ideal of a fully comprehensive resolution of the narrative's elements that he would measure its relative success as a work.

Analogously, personal stories and the degree of one's personal success are evaluated based on the entirety of a person's intentional life. Obviously, the whole novel or movie or play is accessible to us in its entirety while the entirety of somebody's intentional life is not. Still, provided we know somebody well enough, we can discern when he is acting in a manner that can be expected to undermine the coordination of his life. We might spot something he does that obstructs and therefore subtracts from his overall success. In that sense, just as literary critics may have good reasons for judging a novel successful, people sometimes have good reasons for making judgments about others' personal success.

(3) Narrative resolve and personal resolve both purport to achieve the optimal coordination of whatever range of movement it is accountable to.

If a conventional storyteller wants us to take his work seriously, he has to tell his story as well as he can, avoiding episodes that don't ring true, plot developments that go nowhere, poorly developed characters, and irrelevant details. Such flaws may creep in, of course, but if we are to believe that he is genuinely trying to resolve the action of his story we have to assume he is bearing true to that outcome and telling it as well as he can.

Analogously, we maintain, personal storytellers purport to be coordinating their (somatically indexed) intentional lives as well as their imagination enables them. Just as purporting to tell the story as well as one can is part of what it means to be a storyteller, purporting to project the most comprehensive coordination of one's intentional life is implicit in what it means to be personally resolved.

But why is it that personal resolve has to aim for optimal success in this way? We can answer this question by simply recalling that the whole point of resolving one's intentional life is to satisfy as much of it as possible: the more of it being satisfied, the more actualized we are as agents. As multi-intentioned agents, being resolved propels us toward the most satisfying life. We coordinate our lives better in that projection than any other way we can imagine going forward. We follow, if you will, an ontological agenda, an agenda of actualizing ourselves most by telling the most comprehensive personal story we can imagine.

(4) With regard to both narrative resolve and personal resolve, the assessments we make of their relative success are reasonable.

We noted earlier that we expect critics of conventional stories in their various forms to justify the judgments they make about a storyteller's success. The same holds for judgments about relative personal success. People are generally aware when they are doing something that defeats their resolve. We understand what the apostle Paul meant when he said, "I do not understand what I do. For what I want to do I do not do, but what I hate I do." Our ability to distinguish actions lying outside and contrary to our resolve from those within and supportive of it gives us grounds for assessing the gap between the entirely of our agency and our current resolve. But are they *rational* grounds?

To represent our intuitive judgment of someone's relative personal success as rational, we need to make explicit what metric we are using to compare the sphere of somebody's resolute action with the greater sphere of the action of the somatic body he is. Only if we use some standard of comparison can our assessment count as rational.

We testify to using a metric of comparison when we claim to deliberate before making important choices, when we weigh our options. We weigh, one against another, the intentional satisfaction promised by each choice. We ponder them; we ask which way forward promises to satisfy us most, to actualize us most. What this suggests is that the metric we use for comparison is the moment of satisfaction, that is, the active moment in which we actualize our intentions.

Think of it this way. Every accomplishment comprises a range of movement. The measure of any course of accomplishment registers as (what we imagine to be) the combined moments of moving its intended satisfactions. That measure of relative moment is what makes it reasonable to find some accomplishments of greater moment than others and to judge of some that they are truly momentous. So, deliberation can shape the character of our resolve in a rational way given its quest for greatest actualization, which is why we sometimes use 'A did C deliberately' and 'A did C resolutely' interchangeably.

Notice how the process of imaginatively weighing the moments of our options gets distorted by causal language. Richard Taylor was honest enough to acknowledge his puzzlement when he proposed an alternative to "speaking of agents as causing their own acts…[I]t would perhaps be better to use another word entirely, and say, for instance, that they *originate* them, *initiate* them, or simply *perform* them." [10] Notice how Taylor's suggestions strain to get around causal language's treatment of an action as happening at a certain time. The words he prefers, "originate," "initiate," and "perform," all resist punctuality and suggest that acts ought to be considered progressions. To "originate" or "initiate" C is to "launch into a sequence that will accomplish C." To "perform" C is to "carry C through to completion."

But, instead of recognizing the temporal distinctiveness of those more plausible verbs, Taylor defers by default to the logic of cause and effect and is forced to give up trying to account for deliberation altogether.

> No one seems able to describe deliberation without metaphors, and the conception of a thing's being 'within one's power' or 'up to him'

---

[10] Taylor, Richard (1974) *Metaphysics*, 4th edition. Upper Saddle River, NJ: Prentice-Hall, p. 418.

seems to defy analysis or definition altogether if taken in a sense that the theory of agency appears to require.

But if we think of deliberation as happening in the active moment of resolving one's action, because that act is of the character of the person one is, Taylor's problem does not arise.

We deliberate by first comparing courses of action and deciding which one weighs the most in terms of moments of satisfaction. Consider the following soliloquy: "I'll use my frequent flyer miles on next month's trip to Chicago and spend the ticket savings on good restaurants. But no, the flights to Chicago next month are pretty cheap, so maybe I should hold onto my miles and use them to fly to Europe next summer." Each of the two alternatives satisfies and disappoints: Saving the miles opens up my summer prospects but ratchets down restaurant plans; redeeming them now means living lavishly next month but complicating next summer's prospects. We register such scenarios of satisfaction according to how much momentary satisfaction each seems (to our imagination) to import into our prospects.

But though we may start by choosing between alternatives our goal of optimizing our satisfaction often requires us to modify that path to accommodate when possible the advantages of the rejected choice. Imagine that our senator is trying to decide whether she should go to her daughter's high school graduation ceremony or an important fundraiser scheduled for the same day. She has usually been able to balance her professional life with being a mother, but now she's confronted with an unavoidable conflict. Two elements of her personal resolve—to be a good mother and to be a successful politician—dictate mutually incompatible courses. Since she can't be in two places at once, there is no way to coordinate those two courses. She has to choose. But that choice doesn't end her deliberation. After she decides which function to attend we would expect her to minimize the dissatisfaction she is bound to bring about by her choice. If she resolves in favor of her daughter's graduation ceremony, she might also resolve to arrange for a closed-circuit video appearance explaining her support for family values to the fund-raiser. In speaking from the site of her daughter's graduation her absence from the fundraiser might even have some positive value! Or, if the political stakes are so high that she feels compelled to disappoint her daughter, she is likely to think of ways to offset that disappointment, perhaps by promising a belated graduation celebration after the election.

Notice that in exercising the capacity to optimize intentional satisfaction we use our awareness of which intentions are being satisfied and which are not. This suggests that having the capacity to deliberate rationally means having the capacity to judge rationally whether somebody is warranted in purporting to be optimally resolved in the course he projects. That warrant, being a condition for counting as a person, is worth singling out for celebration, so let us distinguish it as acting in *good faith*. A person in good faith is someone who acts with thoughtful deliberation on the testimony of his active imagination with the intention of being as momentously actualized as possible. To project one's life without such honest deliberation, we will say, is to act in *bad faith*.

The four analogies we have been discussing—those between personal resolve and narrative resolve—are widely appreciated among ethicists, theologians, psychiatrists and others who put narrative understandings of persons to effective use. Yet the analogies by themselves do not yield an adequate account of personal identity for forensic purposes. At least two crucial differences between narrative resolve and personal resolve make a purely analogical narrative account of personal identity unreliable.

The first difference is a simple matter of the tense structure of the action related in conventional and personal stories. Conventional stories are told entirely in the past tense:

> Cinderella, who saw all this, and knew that it was her slipper, said to them, laughing, "Let me see if it will not fit me." Her sisters burst out laughing, and began to banter with her. The gentleman who was sent to try the slipper looked earnestly at Cinderella, and, finding her very handsome, said that it was only just that she should try as well, and that he had orders to let everyone try.

Even when a conventional story's action extends into the future it gets related in the past tense: "and they lived happily ever after."

In contrast, we have to use all three tenses to characterize personal resolve. We have seen that the action we project in any given moment of resolve represents the coordination of our present tense intentions in a course of future action the plotting of which depends in large part upon a legacy of earlier moments of resolve whose fruitful patterns of intention-accommodation still promise to sustain our success in the present. That embeds at least some of our earlier moments of resolve in the character of our present resolve, a past to furnish our present projects with strategies for integration that promise to continue to sustain us in good faith.

We should emphasize that the reason for articulating a past as well as the present and future in resolving our actions is a purely practical one. It would be debilitating for somebody to start from scratch in projecting his resolve. Among his present undertakings there are sure to be some that were begun in the past and are still being advanced toward completion. So, if patterns of coordinating these have been established and if those patterns promise to continue serving him, it would be self-defeating to ignore them in favor of *de novo* improvisation.

Accordingly, since we understand ourselves to be advancing a sequence of past moments of resolve it follows that we emerge imaginatively each as the protagonist of a personal story, one begun in a past that continues to inform our present task of projecting a future configured to resolve our present undertakings better than any others. So, unlike characters in a conventional story, we are characters of past, present, and future action.

The second difference between a personal story and a conventional one has to do with the accord or discord we find among the character claims that make it up. A conventional story relates both contentions among actions and a resolution of those contentions. In contrast, since what a person resolves is the satisfaction of the intentions ingredient in his resolve, his resolute projection into the future represents only concordance. The mutually modified ways he projects satisfying his intentions are designed to make them *comportable,* that is to say, *able to be carried along together* to their satisfaction in the course he resolves upon.

In summary: A person can be identified as a character of personal resolve as it—the character of resolve—emerges in storytelling of a distinctive sort. He is born in an imaginative feat that projects his present undertakings into an active future where they find the comportability that achieves their greatest satisfaction. That projection finds solutions to new challenges partly by employing episodes of past resolve that sustain time-tested solutions and partly by imagining new modifications and strategies. The character claims that tell such a story fix a person's identity as the character of a person's resolve in that logically odd sort of story—odd not just for its distinctive tense structure but for its distinctive function, that of resolving the storyteller as a person in good faith.

Taking narrative accounts seriously

We warned above that unless we pay attention to the dis-analogies as well as the analogies between conventional and personal narratives we risk being led astray when we use them to account for personal identity. The ways we risk being led astray can be found in some of the standard criticisms to which narrative accounts of personal identity are thought vulnerable. A glance at a few of them will show why they do not constitute a significant challenge to the account being proposed.

One hears it said that any person identified by a story would be fated to live out a predetermined course of action the way those tragic figures in the Greek stories did. It is possible, we concede, to entertain the idea that one's life is fated—the way the Ancient Greeks apparently did—but surely most of us would resist interpreting our lives that way. Somebody who believed that his life was entirely worked out in advance would probably seem mentally ill to us, his story best told on an analyst's couch. (Indeed, Freudian case studies are among the few tragic narratives available after Shakespeare.) In any case, this criticism does not apply to our account since personal stories are not the kind of stories whose actions are all past-tensed.

Another complaint is that narrative accounts of identity represent just the sort of illegitimate hegemony of one story over others that postmodernity is meant to deliver us from. No one can doubt that there are numerous narratives informing how we understand our action, so, the allegation goes, they provide a patchwork of "identities," not identity as an individual. That being the case, we are often advised to give up on the age-old practice of identifying persons as individuals and think of people as protean shape-shifters.

But what this advice overlooks is the peculiar role one story has over others in sustaining our good faith. Certainly, there are many narrative models suggestive of ways we might successfully conduct elements of our intentional life, but we should not ignore the one we project to resolve our action nor should we deny its proper hold over us. For as long as our present personal story resolves us best, we are accountable for advancing it coherently—or at least not impeding it—by what we do.

Finally, there is another version of anti-narrativity that assumes that narrative accounts of identity commit us to a diachronic model of personhood rather than one that is entirely in the present. Galen Strawson, for instance, calls the being of a person "Episodic," and assumes that "if you're Episodic you're not Narrative."[11] What is so appealing about the Episodic person—to Strawson and most of the rest of us too—is that it frees us to think of ourselves as wholly in the present. There is a sense of liberation in this since the diachronic interpretation of identity prevents robust personal presence from being fully interpretable. In fact, we suspect that much of the appeal of postmodernism traces to a celebration of the victory of the Episodic over the Diachronic.

But Strawson's claim that what is Episodic cannot be Narrative is unwarranted. Our account finds the entire being of a person implicit in the present character of his resolve—episodic rather than diachronic—yet it finds that only a narrative can disclose the meaning of that presence. So while Strawson captures our resolute presence appropriately in the word "Episodic" he mis-

---

[11] Galen Strawson, "Against Narrativity" in *Ratio (new series)* XVII 4 December 2004, p. 432.

takenly thinks that only chronological time can host a personal story. That leads him to deny that the active present pulls as its past a supply train of moments of resolve feeding the narrative capacities we use to project our future wisely now.

We cannot fully retrieve narrativity from the strictures of chronological thinking until we explore what is included in someone's present moment of resolve, so we turn next to the distinctive temporality of active presence.

Chapter 2

Personal Presence

We have been discussing the reigning consensus among students of human behavior about what counts as reasoning about actors and actions. It is one that largely decommissions "person" from systematic service (along with other rusty hulks of a once mighty metaphysical fleet). Yet we still think of ourselves as reasoning about persons in everyday life, reasoning about them in ways that are crucial to the success of our interactions. We identify and address people personally, show them personal respect, accord them personal rights, hold them personally responsible and make personal promises, and we make these interactive moves with some confidence that we know who we are dealing with. Moreover, we think we have reasons for holding someone personally responsible (or not responsible, or irresponsible) and for judging that he was (or was not) within his personal rights. We think of ourselves as reasonable in making such forensic judgments because we see them as grounded in evidence and we know how to draw reasonable conclusions from such evidence.

Our era's loss of confidence that we can reason about persons strikes us as curious but also alarming, alarming because unless we can give a reasonable account of the scope of somebody's personal agency—and thus the range of action wherein he acts with personal responsibility and wherein he is within his personal rights—we can no longer defend moral and legal judgments as rational. For a time the inertia of the superannuated idea of personal agency may continue to support the honoring of personal respect, but eventually, one has to suspect, the unanswered question of identity will erode the protocols of that respect. If "person" is dismissed as a vestigial conceit inherited from a discredited folk psychology, eventually we must expect the ideology of a person-respecting and person-fostering society to be in danger.

Goaded by that dismal prospect and convinced that it need not be our fate, we have launched this recovery-of-the-person operation with an examination of some of the inferences we make about actions and agents. We found that the form a character claim must take if it is to identify a person is the form a claim takes when it advances a personal story. We found too that this forward-in-time projection toward intentional resolution depends for its stability on the projector's identification with certain earlier moments of his resolve, the ones that inform how he coordinates his life now. For as long as those earlier moments of resolve are in narrative continuity with his present resolve they constitute his past; by extension, so too do other of his past acts that accorded in those past moments of resolve. They are all part of who he was and is. We concluded then that a person's active being includes those past actions that allow his present resolve to be figured as an advance in the story of his optimal resolve.

This chapter picks up on the peculiar temporality such story-shaped characters inhabit. Exploring that temporal frame for personal existence will enable us to make better sense of what we find distinctive in a person's presence, particularly his interactive presence. We saw earlier that personal presence has the character of resolve and that any character of resolve projects an active future in narrative continuity with certain past moments of resolve. It follows that no person could be present to himself or to others unless he registered temporally in all three tenses. We can confirm our intuitive sense of this three-fold requirement if we try to imagine an agent missing any one of them. If somebody had no apparent coordination in his intentional life, his intentions would not bear individual character, which is the condition for being a person. If somebody had no awareness of his past he would (if movie clichés about amnesia sufferers are believable) be intent on recovering it as a way of discovering who he is. If somebody showed no signs of caring about anything beyond his immediate occupation, the resolve required for personal presence would be lacking. That is why Dante put the irresolute in a vestibule to hell. They were not quite the kind of being who could qualify as a subject of God's condemnation.

This three-fold temporal registry of personal presence helps us understand something else that otherwise tends to be conceptually elusive, the momentary variability we find in one another's presence. When people are generous in what they disclose of their intentional lives, they are more richly and deeply present with us. So too are those seen to be embarked on momentous undertakings. For a long time it has been difficult for Westerners to come to terms with this momentary variability because of their ancient metaphysical commitment to the notion of substance. This is because when we represent the being of a person as the being of a substance we make personal presence a binary matter. Substances are either present or they are not. If persons are substantial selves their being is either present or absent.

Now that the binary yoke is off, one might hope that a philosophical appreciation of presence has been liberated. But this has not happened. English speaking analytic philosophers who have investigated identity issues ignore variable presence because they follow Locke and Hume in accepting the challenge as one of determining the range of *experiences* it makes sense to count as those of a given person. There are, according to this line of inquiry, two general ways to set the range of a given person's experiences. One could choose to treat a given person's experiences as all of his experiences over his lifetime (the so-called four-dimensionalist position associated with David Lewis and John Perry) or one could choose to treat only his present experiences as properly who he is (the position that persuaded Derek Parfit to retire "person" from any important role in moral and legal discourse). Neither of these ways of marking the boundaries of a person's being proves conducive to making sense of momentary variability. Under the first option, since most of anyone's past is likely to have fallen into oblivion, one could have only a very thin personal presence; under the second option, a person—attenuated as the concept will have become—is fully present (at least to himself) all of the time, which outflanks relative presence from the other direction.

On the other side of the English Channel, variable personal presence—indeed any kind of presence—is widely dismissed on the grounds of the contingency of all meaning. Contingency (the dominant view contends) makes any significance different from what it purports to signify, making the very idea of the presence of one character with another incoherent.

The way to avoid these dead-ends is to recognize that the appropriate logic of presence is the one governing *active* presence. It is the temporal logic governing character claims that must be used to interpret presence. When we grasp the moment of somebody's personal presence as a moment of his active presence, it makes perfectly good sense to understand interactive presence as presence in a shared moment. Because the interactors are *in* the active moment together, they are (momentarily) present *with* one another. And, since their interactive accomplishment can be of greater or lesser magnitude, so too can the momentary value of their presence with each other.

Now, armed with this preliminary re-reading of momentary presence—whether with oneself or with others—we think we can gain the leverage we need to determine the active scope of a person and the volume of his presence. There are, let us suggest, three ways to measure the movement being determined by the present character of somebody's resolve: by measuring the moments of his intentional life that it comprehends, by measuring the movement that it characterizes in the actions of other people, and by measuring its historical importance. When we factor these three together the distinctive variability of personal presence gets accounted for, but before we can factor these dimensions of personal moment we need to consider our awareness of each of them separately.

Persons are present in the accord in their individual lives

One measure of somebody's personal presence is the relative success he has in executing his intentional life in accord with his resolve. Imagine what might count as the elements of somebody's intentional life. Presumably, each of us could, upon reflection, make a sizable list of present-continuing intentional undertakings, including some immediate ventures (I'm reading this sentence), some ongoing undertakings (I'm reading *The Brothers Karamazov*), and some others that are mostly on the drawing board (I'm planning to visit the Balkans this spring). Presumably our lists will also include personal relationships we are sustaining, institutional commitments we are living out, hobbies, business ventures, retirement plans, vocational aspirations, and all the other projections we make of our movement into the future.

But, as we saw earlier, it is not just by having these intentions that one is the person one is. One is that person because of how he balances all these interests by resolving how he projects their satisfactions comportably.

Imagine now that you know someone well enough to grasp something of how he is making room for everything, accommodating himself to what is most important and modifying what is less important so that, generally speaking, his life is one of accord. If you knew him well enough to grasp that active core, you would probably discover that there were at least some things he did that didn't accord with his resolve. Occasionally you might catch him acting thoughtlessly, using language hurtfully, or maybe in some bigger way "yielding to temptation." Sometimes, in other words, you become aware of him momentarily dropping his resolve long enough to indulge certain wayward intentions. And one thing we can say about these wayward intentions on formal grounds is that they represent depletions in his being as a character of resolve. They represent moments subtracted from the body of his resolve.

Notice that our ability to distinguish actions falling within a person's resolve from actions counteracting it suggests as a paradigm of personhood a core of resolve functioning within the greater body of his intentional life. In this model somebody's resolve can register as relatively comprehensive of his agency. It follows that one basis we have for assessing a person's relative success is a measure of how comprehensive his resolve is.

In the pages ahead it is going to be important to get clear about how we measure the core of agency we accredit as a particular person. The way we want to approach this problem is by observing how a personal core of presence would character logically have to emerge in somebody's agency. Personhood is not present from birth and it sometimes never develops, but if it does develop it does so of logical necessity in a series of steps, steps required to develop the imaginative prowess needed to sustain active self-awareness as an individual character of resolve.

Given what we discovered in the last chapter about the narrative structure of that resolve it seems reasonable to expect that the prowess involved in forming personal resolve will prove closely related to the capacity to tell a story. It is also reasonable to expect that the series of imaginative feats a developing agent has to master before he can project himself as an individual character of resolve are narrative feats. So then, our strategy for tracing the developmental sequence from infancy through childhood and from adolescence into individual personhood will be to look at the types of narratives we have to master at various stages along the way.

At the most fundamental level, somebody's action is identifiable as such because it is determined by an intention. Moreover, we assume that that intention is somehow figured in the active awareness of its agent. The sequence of movements we recognize as an action is assumed to be coordinated by an active awareness of that intention. "Look, she's crawling to Grandma!" means more than "Look, she's moving in Grandma's direction!" It means that some primitive feat is occurring in her active imagination enabling her to *in-tend*, *stretch-into*, her bearing...all the way to Grandma. She *meant* to crawl to Grandma, we say, and to *mean* is to have in mind, thus to mean to do something is to coordinate one's movements around a character of action one has in mind.

Another thing it seems safe to say about the form of an infant's active awareness is that it is single-minded, mono-intentional. As full-fledged persons we are multi-intentioned agents, but babies do only one thing at a time. They are serial actors, not multi-taskers. And that is as it must be. An agent cannot do many things at once until he has learned to do one thing at a time. Evidence for infantile single-mindedness can be seen and heard in the completeness of a baby's disappointment when the one thing he is doing is frustrated. With his one and only intention thwarted, he is completely annihilated as an agent and since he is thus utterly consumed by dissatisfaction, he can, as an agent, only "break down," dissolve into primal rage.

So there is a ground zero of momentary being. But agency quickly reasserts itself and some moment is achieved. The development of an infant's agency starts with mastering accomplishments of progressively greater duration (building a wall, not just stacking two blocks; drawing a picture, not just scribbling). As the accomplishments become more movement-comprehensive, they yield greater actuality to him as an agent. And since it is the nature of agency to satisfy intentions, satisfying more intentions is the way we grow. We thus strive to increase the moment of our actions from the very beginning. Our being, our agentive being, is movement toward the satisfaction of intentions. The more moments of intentional satisfaction we achieve, the more actualized we are. It follows that becoming more actualized for a human means determining more movement in the character of what one is doing.

If we look at this in terms of the infant's active awareness we see that new levels of prowess are called for if the development is to proceed. Learning to *mean* actions in longer and longer arcs of coordinated movement requires the ability to project those longer arcs. And here is where stories are crucial. They are the natural vehicles for learning to act on a bigger scale.

And what kind of stories serve at this level? To begin where the infant is, one must tell a story of sustained movement in the service of a single intention—the little engine that could, going to a birthday party, helping Grandma to bake cookies. Such stories stretch the character of movement toward the satisfaction of an intention, so following such stories gives a child practice in coordinating greater ranges of movement to satisfy intentions of greater moment.

With success in increasing the momentary actualization of what he is aware of doing, a different sort of challenge becomes inevitable. The longer it takes to do something the more intrusions are likely to stymie the doing of it as it was originally intended. That calls for a course correction, which is why a baby needs next to be exposed to stories where unanticipated developments block the ways originally projected and make it necessary to improvise. For example, a story about going on a picnic is complicated by an unexpected thunderstorm, so the picnic has to be moved indoors … but it proves to be fun anyway.

The satisfaction of longer form intentions, in addition to being subject to revision due to unexpected eventualities, come to be frustrated by contending agents. Little Heather grabs candy from the checkout display; Mom puts it back. Zack wants to stay up; Dad sends him to bed. Since children always negotiate from a position of weakness (in that their intending can determine the character of less movement) it is never a fair struggle. Thus the narrative feat they must manage next is how to interact with vastly more powerful agents: Cinderella by escaping domination by her stepsisters, Hansel and Gretel by tricking the witch, Jack by outfoxing the giant. In each tale a weak protagonist's intention—going to the Royal Ball, escaping from the wicked witch, climbing down the beanstalk—contends with a vastly more powerful agent's intention, contends and somehow prevails.

Of course the "somehow prevails" is facilitated by the enchanted worlds of the stories with the magical solutions they make available, but there is also another reason so many children's stories enchant the action, one that has to do with the epistemic priority active awareness has over their awareness of natural events. Children are largely innocent about how things unfold in the real world. Theirs is an actual realm first, and in a purely actual realm nothing precludes fairy godmothers from casting spells, animals from talking, or beanstalks from growing into the sky.

In that priority—of understanding actuality before understanding reality— the cognitive development of a baby can be said to recapitulate that of the species. The first storytellers also understood what happened in vividly actual but highly unrealistic ways. They told of gods summoning sweet zephyrs to lull lovers, smart breezes to propel safe passage, and raging storms to wreck a disfavored warrior's ship. What is common to such narrative worlds and the worlds of young children is that everything important happens intentionally. In a word, they are supernatural worlds.

One could say too that for children and ancient people alike enchantment had comparable tutorial utility: the character of any act cuts a more intelligible figure for the imagination when there are no natural impediments to its accomplishment. The resistance of nature to agency in the real world complicates the intended course of just about any momentous accomplishment. That makes narrating it realistically too complicated for a child's imagination or a prescientific imagination to follow. For the unpracticed imagination, simplifying eventualities for the sake of better characterizing actualities puts the character of more momentous action within cognitive reach.

But the uses of enchantment have their developmental limits. Children will need to take events into account in order to act successfully when they experience unrealistic intentions being frustrated. That is why good parents admonish a child to "grow up!" when he acts less realistically than they think he can and should, and why a child's eventual need to negotiate a real world as well as an actual one leads older children to find realistic stories increasingly compelling. In biographies, adventure stories, sports stories, and celebrity stories children explore worlds where unintentional forces (as well as intentional ones) propel or frustrate people's purposes. In following them they nourish imaginative prowess to meet real-world challenges for the sake of meeting actual-world challenges. Again, it is, if you will, an ontological lure drawing forth this development by holding out the promise of ever-more momentous being. Becoming realistic is simply another necessary step in enriching and extending one's intentional life.

But notice, the realistic stories older children crave are not at first personal stories; they are told to characterize actions only within a particular precinct of a protagonist's life. In the early days of television, youngsters avidly followed the adventures of "The Lone Ranger" who brought law and order to the Old West. But that's about all there was to him. For those kids, that relative intentional simplicity was just fine since they weren't inclined to ask whether he had a love life, a religious life, or a retirement plan. The same is true for other heroes like Luke Skywalker. (Worth noting is that the adventures of the Lone Ranger have continued to excite viewers, with movies made in 1961, 1981, 2003, and 2013).

Eventually, though, another practicality forces every multi-intentioned agent to recognize that for the sake of their greatest actualization they need a character of resolve that ranges over the entirety of their intentional life, or over at least as much of it as they can imagine. They are thus challenged to project their individuality as an agent in that form, challenged to resolve themselves by becoming personal storytellers.

If adolescence begins when somebody first tries to resolve his intentional life as a whole, it ends when he feels reasonably warranted in purporting to tell a story that does just that as well as it can. And here too the stories he now finds useful reflect his developmental challenge. The literary imagination most needed to meet it is one that projects a protagonist who achieves successful personal resolution. Such stories might suggest tropes for an adolescent's own negotiation of an overall coordination. Stories of this sort fall into the genre of the *Bildungsroman*, as illustrated by Goethe's *The Apprenticeship of Wilhelm Meister*. More recent examples include J. D. Salinger's *The Catcher in the Rye* and several novels adapted for film, including John Irving's *The Cider House Rules*, Nick Hornby's *About a Boy*, Sue Monk Kidd's *The Secret Life of Bees*, and Khaled Hosseini's *The Kite Runner*. All of these works reveal the challenges of being accountable to one's resolve and chronicle the ways in which the respective protagonists move beyond adolescence.

When one considers how formidable the challenge is likely to be, it is hardly surprising that adolescence is a turbulent stage. Not only are there contentious impositions posed by events and other people, but there is also a keener awareness of the contentions within. An adolescent learns to be accountable to his intentional life as a whole only after many unwise forays and painful retreats, false starts and setbacks. But, since what is at stake is nothing less than his greatest success as a complex intentional being, when self-defeating plans have been abandoned and bruises healed, he will try again until he finds some *modus vivendi* that holds his life together in good faith. Again, it is that abiding ontological lure to maximize our moment that prompts us to learn to tell a personal story. It is in that narrative achievement that a child becomes an individual, someone with identity in a person-respecting, person-fostering society. As we will see, for moral and legal purposes this passage is the one whereby an adolescent becomes someone with personal rights and personal responsibilities and thus, forensically, an adult.

In the chapters ahead we are going to see how personal rights and responsibilities are grounded in an agent's status as an individual character of resolve. But first, for symmetry's sake and to observe how this way of reasoning informs other of our intuitions, we will retrace our steps in the opposite direction and take note of how the same stages of personal being are marked along the road to dissolution. The way up and the way down are the same. A person emerges by way of someone's active integration and dies in his active disintegration.

On the way up, there was first behavior without agency, then childhood agency with little moment, then, with more complexity of intentional life, greater moment, and finally the imaginative achievement of an individual character of resolve. On that plateau of personal maturity, the stage we strut and fret our hour upon, we are both the storyteller of and the protagonist in the distinctive kind of tale we are calling a personal story. When the maintenance of one's character individuality becomes impossible—as it must for us all eventually—one stops sustaining it and dies as a bearer of personal rights and responsibilities. He enters into what is aptly called a "second childhood," no longer present as the richly resolved individual character he once was. He is now what Josiah Royce called a "person by courtesy," an agent we treat with kindness for the sake of the person he was. (We will return to the question of what rights and responsibilities we have relative to such people in chapter 4.)

Finally there is death. Sometimes the death of a person precedes the death of his body, as we have been discussing, and sometimes they happen together. But since they can constitute different occasions, there is at least a logical possibility we need to explore. Is it conceivable that a person could live on after his body's death? That is, does the character logic of identity allow for that possibility?

We raise this question because when we frame it as one about a subject of action rather than a subject of experience we can see some ways our intuitions about personal destiny are being informed, even as they are being denigrated by the reigning category logic about persons. Where that reign has not become entirely hegemonic, the somatically deceased often continue to be present in person for at least a time, sometimes to commune with the living. The Mexican Day of the Dead, for example, celebrates continuing personal presence, as do the beliefs and practices of some contemporary African cultures.[12]

---

[12] David A. Hoekema, "African Personhood: Morality and Identity in the 'Bush of Ghosts'," *Soundings* 91.3-4 (Fall/Winter 2008).

To intellectually sophisticated people, belief in the lingering presence of the dead is likely to be regarded as superstition. They would insist that we cannot reasonably take such beliefs seriously. But consider that only a few generations separate us from our ancestors' hauntings by the recently deceased (think of Hamlet and Scrooge). Even today, some of those who regard it irrational can be found communing at a loved one's grave site. The intuition cannot be entirely smothered. That is because our intuition of a person as a character of resolve allows us to re-configure belief in the presence of the dead as belief in the presence of ongoing resolve.

When a friend or family member dies, it is likely that some of what he was resolved to do will have been left undone, including perhaps undertakings that were important to him. His true friends may then feel obliged to carry out his resolve, completing what they can in order to "tie things up." Why so? Once having formed a partnership with the person who subsequently died, they often adopt his resolve as a governor over their actions until his most resolved intentions are carried out. This adoption is, after all, what made their relationship personal. His resolve set conditions on how they acted out their own intentions. Each of them undertook to actualize himself in accord with how the other resolved his life in good faith.

Though he is now dead as a subject of experience, the matter of his continuing presence as a character of resolve is not necessarily settled. If the achievement of what he was resolved to do continues to be advanced by his friends their actions represent movement in his personal character. "He would have wanted me to contact his family, find a home for his dogs, see his manuscript into print, and sell his business." The result of discharging this obligation to enact what was crucial in a partner's resolve is that the living partners get to dwell a while longer in that personal resolve. Because their movement can be said to actualize him momentarily when they bring elements of his resolve to completion, he is, in that moment, with them as a character of resolve, therefore, as a person.

By being faithful to the deceased, the still-living friend is made freer to "let go," to separate his life. And that is good for both parties. Old Marley's ghost and that of Hamlet's father both summoned a former partner who was in a position to carry out some yet undone, momentous element in his resolve, for only then could they be accomplished enough to rest in peace. And, in carrying out those resolutions, Scrooge and Hamlet became more secure in their own identities.[13]

---

[13] We are leaving aside any discussion of religious beliefs about personal destiny. That topic is discussed in Richard C. Prust's *Wholeness: the Character Logic of Christian Belief* (Amsterdam and New York: Rodopi Press, 2004).

We have been tracing the stages a multi-intentioned being has to pass through in order to emerge as a person and then to dissolve as one. The point of tracing the arc of personal being has been to get clearer about the boundaries of a person's presence. Because it makes sense to denominate presence in terms of moment, and because moments can, in principle, be measured, our personal presence can be said to have volume according to how much of our life is being comprehended by our resolve. But you will recall that in addition to the moment of the resolution of somebody's intentional life there are two other realms of momentary movement actualizing his character. There are whatever added moments of movement his resolve actualizes in others' lives, and there is the future importance of what he and they actively advance. All three volumes figure into the magnitude of a person's moment, so, having discussed the first, we now turn to the second and third.

Persons are present in the lives of others in the moments of their interaction

Persons are interactively present in the character of others' actions, the more so when their interaction is personal. While the social nature of human beings has been widely acknowledged, it has been regarded within the tradition dominated by category logic merely as a remarkable fact. As long as Western intellectuals thought of persons as individual substances, interpersonal relationships were considered contingent facts about them, not active contributions to their very identity. Retrieving the character logic we have retained in ordinary reasoning allows us better to understand the ways in which our lives, and even our destinies, are intertwined. Character logically, one party can intend a character of action moved by the other's accomplishments as well as his own.

But while we all know what it means to be with another person in a way that momentarily resolves our individualities interactively, that intuitive sense has been sublimated to the detriment of clear forensic thinking. As Carol Gilligan observed, "the voice that set the dominant key in ... law and in ethics, was keyed to separation: the separate self, the individual acting alone, the possessor of natural rights, the autonomous moral agent."[14]

To better align our reason with our intuition (so that we can understand how persons get actualized in each other's lives) it should help to highlight our everyday awareness of interactively extending our resolve into another's movement. On the most obvious level, one might think of a boss and the un-

---

[14] Carol Gilligan, "Hearing the Difference: Theorizing Connection," Hypatia, vol. 10, no. 2 (Spring 1995).

derling who does his bidding. The latter moves according to the resolve of the former, who pays him for his movement.

But of course (one hopes) not many of our relations are so one-sided in character determination. Consider the following example: A chef and sous-chef are preparing a dinner. They only know one another professionally, not outside the kitchen. Their togetherness is impersonal. But within their shared domain they strive to move in a highly coordinated way. To achieve that working relation, each must make allowances for how the other plays his role. The chef is called the chef because he specifies in general terms how the sous-chef will operate. But the sous-chef's peculiar strengths and weaknesses call for modifications on the chef's part, like deciding what elements of the preparation to hand off and which ones to take upon himself. In moving together with a common intention, each modifies how the other moves.

Let us imagine that tonight the meal they prepared for us was unusually delightful. What made their success memorable was more than the sum of their separate talents; it was how they brought them into harmony around their joint accomplishment. The mutual inflection of each other's character of action redounded to the greater success of what they achieved together. And because their interaction actualized each of them more than either could have been actualized on his own, it too represents a response to the ontological prompting for an agent who seeks to maximize his individual moment of intentional satisfaction.

If it is true that in any healthy interaction our inflection of one another's movement actualizes greater moment in us both, that is all the more pronounced when the interaction is personal. Then we inflect not just the other's moves in some specific cooperative undertaking but the whole being of the other as a character of resolve that we are jointly committed to achieving! In that sense, friends inhabit one another's actions more fully than the chefs did. That is why friends seem to actualize themselves more in each other's presence.

How much we inhabit one another as persons varies in volume according to how many elements of each other's resolve we are aware of. Consider the following scenario: Jay is at a party with his friends Dee, Kay, Em and you. Some in your group know Jay better than others. Dee, for instance, senses that Jay is resolved to leave the party early. She caught him glancing at the clock repeatedly, and that prompted her to recall what she noticed when she drove up, that he was parked on the street and not in the driveway as usual. Now it dawns on her that he parked there to avoid getting blocked in. She's hardly surprised because she knows that he needs to get an early morning start on his drive to a job interview. She reads his early departure as an accommodation to getting a good night's sleep before a big day.

You too have been watching Jay's action, and you too put two and two together. His frequent time checks and the fact that he is parked on the street also tell you that he is determined to leave the party early. And, sure enough, just as you predicted, at about 10:30 Jay bids his hosts goodnight and makes his way out into the night. You and Dee both understand his action in terms of his resolve, but, unlike Dee, you know nothing about the job interview. Dee understands the character of Jay's action more richly than you do.

But look! There's Em, Jay's sister. She knows what Dee knows, but she also knows that Jay's main reason for coming to the party tonight was to see Bea. Since Bea was one of the last people to arrive, Em could see frustration in Jay's glances at the time, but even Em doesn't know that Jay has already determined to call Bea tomorrow after the job interview. Still, the character of Jay's action as Em is aware of it turns out to be even richer than Dee's.

There is not much interaction in this little scenario but we can nonetheless see how the variability of interactive presence would be conditioned by the richness of one's awareness of the other's resolve. But now let's imagine that more than a decade has passed. Instead of just being casual friends at a party Jay and Bea are married and joyously toasting their tenth wedding anniversary. Old college friends Dee, Kay, and you are there to celebrate along with sister Em. Having been married for all that time, Jay and Bea have become well-tuned not only to the idiosyncrasies in the other's intentional life but to the complex and ever-shifting equilibrium of their conviviality. Each is committed to honor the resolve of the other in how he or she conducts their relationship. Over the years they have both learned to execute the bulk of what they individually undertake in preservation of that harmony, so much so that they sometimes think of themselves as sharing one life.

So it seems reasonable to say then that over the decade of their growing togetherness Jay and Bea each actualized moments of satisfaction in the other in a way that extended the active being of each. Their healthy relationship was to both of them a telic accomplishment—a response to the ontological prompt to increase one's moment.

Personal presence extends into the lives of future persons

Persons, our account suggests, are present in the future importance of what they do. This is the third dimension of moments determined in character by what we do resolutely. We inflect the character of future accomplishment either to actualize it in greater moment or to deplete its conditions for success. In the former case, the character of our present resolve actualizes moment in that future accomplishment.

Personal historical importance registers in terms of what active possibilities he intends to open up in the lives of those who outlive him. The most obvious example is a parent's awareness of shaping a child's possibilities. For example, parents instill in their children a functional model that will influence the formation of later personal and social relations. Parents also have a lasting influence on their children by fostering imagination, or, alternatively, by stifling imagination. Good parenting creates more momentous possibilities for the child's future life; bad parenting less.

To the extent a parent's resolve creates more moment in the child's future, that creation extends his own being into the future. Inflecting his child's active life facilitates (or inhibits) the creation of future moment in the child's later life. Because a parent can add moment to the child's future actions by how he, the parent, is presently resolved, that legacy can add moment to his personal presence.

The Multiplier Effect in the Three Registers

We have been discussing three ways persons actualize themselves: in their individuality as agents, in the character of their interactivity, and in their future historical importance. Since we are never present in just one of these dimensions of moment, we have to understand a person's presence as a compound of the three.

But rather than being the sum of the three, he is their multiplicative product. This suggests that, if we are to appreciate the limits of a person's agency (for forensic purposes), we should pay heed to how this multiplier effect works. Let us start with an illustration of how historical importance, the third of the three, might depend on the first two dimensions of moment. Imagine someone who has, over many years, filled a huge penny bowl. Imagine further that the filling of the penny bowl was unconnected with anything else in his rich and successful life. Imagine that he started doing it on a whim, then got curious about how long it would take, and pretty soon got into the habit of tossing his pocket change in. Despite the long time it took to fill the bowl, his celebration of the final penny toss would probably be a fairly low-key affair. Despite the fact that the project took him many years, it is not likely to be mentioned in his obituary.

Long-term accomplishments are celebrated as momentous only when they advance either the actor's resolve or his relational life or both. Think of how people traditionally welcome in the New Year by singing with old friends about old friends. On this occasion, people dwell on their experience of time, feeling gratitude for what has gotten them this far in life and making resolutions that they hope will make their future even brighter. When the ritual celebrates the importance of enduring relationships—the second of the three dimensions—it imports greater moment to the occasion. If we are alone on New Year's Eve, the occasion rings with more irony than joy. True, the stroke of midnight registers as vaguely more momentous than did the stroke of 12 the night before, but of itself it seems almost as silly to celebrate as a full penny bowl. The moment moves from ironic to iconic only when it is shared with *auld lang* friends.

Another illustration of the compounding that goes on among the registers of active moment, particularly between the second and third, was suggested to us by a picture from the sports pages during a recent NCAA basketball tournament. Depicting a scene from "March Madness," it showed the Tar Heels roaring out onto the court, high-fiving their way through a gauntlet of gleeful fans. Imagine if you will that you are one of those fans caught by the camera and that you were fully as excited as you look in the picture. For you it was a moment to remember and if some obtuse soul were to ask why you treasured it so much, you would kindly explain that it was just before the championship game, the culmination of the Final Four. The importance of the whole season depended on how Carolina performed that particular night. Notice first how the duration of the accomplishment being undertaken factors into its importance. The scope of "winning the NCAA tournament" includes many more moments of movement than does that of "winning the game."

But its durational scope is only one part of its importance for you. It was all the more important because you were there; you were part of it! There is a big difference between being present at the game and watching it on TV. Why so? Because the awareness of the active moment had an added register for you: the moment was enhanced by the interactivity you lent your movement to. That made you part of the moment in a way the TV viewer, even an avid fan, could not be.

The invigorating interactive presence felt by fans in a stadium or coliseum is sometimes likened to a religious experience. One hears loose talk about sports arenas being the new cathedrals and athletic contests the new services of worship. There is, to be sure, a compelling analogy in that both services of worship and athletic contests involve shared and heightened emotions, ritualized activities, and something like a priesthood presiding. At the same time, however, there are differences: religious rites purport to enact personal relationships among those who are party to them. Even when the participants do not know one another well in real life, they nonetheless acknowledge their common resolve by greeting one another as brothers and sisters. They believe that fellowship is guaranteed by the common action in whose "service" they join. That assurance ideally allows them to cooperate with the kind of trust they extend in their personal friendships.

Something of this sort is also available at sporting events, though generally not to the same degree. Whereas avid fans find themselves unified in spirit, there are always just enough fans of the opposing team to remind everyone that the spirit is not unanimous. Moreover, fans' interactions tend to remain more impersonal. It is unusual, though by no means unheard of, for people who had previously been perfect strangers to embrace in celebration of the team's victory. During a regular season game, especially at professional sports events, spectators observe a decorum that reminds them that they are in fact virtual strangers.

Though they remain strangers, and are not likely to stay in contact following the game, there is nevertheless a fleeting sense of community that approaches that of a religious service. Spectators can inflate their interactive moment by jointly functioning as an accomplice to the team's victory, and for that to happen they must coordinate their movements with the action on the floor or field. At dramatic or decisive junctures of the game, fans' movements are determined in character by the character of what their team is doing. They rise to their feet in unison to cheer, recoil together at bad calls, wince at injuries, and burnish success with hoarse cries. More than simply being aware of the action as keen-eyed spectators, they move in accord with the play and with the intentions of those around them. This amplified interaction makes them aware of being together in a moment they share, the same great moment of the team's accomplishment. For them it feels honest to say, "We pulled for" the team and, "We won," for by moving in the character of the team's action they actually functioned marginally in its success. That is at least one of the reasons athletes enjoy a "home court advantage," why theater actors perform best for a good house, and why musicians encourage audiences to clap or dance to the beat. Participation adds value to the moment because an audience moving with the action inflates its moment in everybody's awareness, including the team's or performer's.

Before we leave behind the athletic examples of compounded moment, there is another analogy between sporting events and religious events that can be instructive. Both seek to make grace manifest. We have seen that the ideal of storytelling is the achievement of perfect resolution. We would add that perfect narrative resolution has a formal kinship with the graceful physical performance an athlete strives for. Both are manifest as having a singularity of character. The physical grace of an alley-oop dunk, the pass perfectly thrown to avoid the outstretched hands of the defenders, is reminiscent of the finest choreography. Even defensive prowess in basketball, football, and soccer, which is often thought of more in terms of toughness than gracefulness, requires instantaneous awareness and coordination on the part of every player on the team. The gracefulness of a skilled basketball team is like the sonic grace of good music, the somatic grace of skilled dancers, and the dramaturgic grace of a good theater company. All of these social activities manifest a level of coordination analogous to the personal and interpersonal health we aim to achieve for ourselves. That, we suspect, is why a secular era in particular finds the performing arts, including sports, so compelling. The graces on display have become the only emblems of active wholeness we can all appreciate.

Given that the volume of someone's personal presence is its active being in all three of its dimensions, our icons of personal achievement must approach ultimate moment. Martin Luther King, Jr.'s "I have a dream" speech and Gandhi's harvest of sea salt were momentously important to many people because each could be construed as an act of integrity advancing a great "movement" in history that rode on an immense interactive coordination of personal effort.

We have been making the case along the way that as multi-intentioned agents we seek to bring ourselves into being as momentously as possible...in the comprehension of our intentional lives, in the wholesomeness of our interactions and in the future importance of what we do. This triumvirate of natural aspirations prompts us to imagine emblems of their conjoined ultimacy and to celebrate places and occasions when someone's actions seemed momentous on all three registers. They guide our search as a kind of natural religion. The Kaaba in Mecca, the grotto in Jerusalem, a Seder meal, a Christian Eucharist: all serve some persons to focus the ultimacy of moment to which all persons naturally aspire.

Our objective in developing this account of personal identity is to show that our reasoning about the character of somebody's resolve determines certain fundamental moral and legal intuitions we tend to honor unless, that is, we veer from the guidance of character logic. When we fall into the habit of identifying persons as individual entities of some sort as opposed to characters of resolve, our reasoning becomes counter-intuitive. But, as we hope to show in the next two chapters, when we remind ourselves of the appropriate way to draw inferences about persons and their actions we can find our way back to our intuitive reasoning.

To test our account we will ask first whether our sense of somebody's present character of resolve informs us when we judge whether he was within his personal rights to have done something. Then we will ask whether that same sense of identity determines someone's personal responsibility for what he does. If these two determinations generally square with our intuitions in these matters and are useful in solving some of the salient puzzles that have arisen about moral and legal issues, our account will have succeeded in recovering "persons" for those purposes.

Chapter 3

Personal Rights

We launched this study with a promise that by observing how we use character claims when we reason our way toward moral and legal judgments we could discern the logic we use to identify those we judge. We found that somebody's present character of resolve has the authority to identify him for as long as it imports the greatest moment into his active awareness. Because a person is an agent—one whose being is to satisfy intentions—and because human agency is multi-intentioned, the resolve someone thinks will actualize him most momentously identifies him as a person.

This understanding of persons puts us in a position to look at some of the ways of identifying them by their resolve determines certain basic rights and responsibilities. The current chapter examines the rights we have by virtue of being characters of resolve. It is not our objective to examine in detail the issues we discuss but only to spotlight certain crucial inferential moves we make in discussing them, moves that bear out the recognition of ourselves and others as individual characters of resolve when we assign rights.

The fundamental right of a person is, by definition, the right to be who he is, that is, to be the character of resolve he presently is. That is both his moral right and, to the extent a society is person-respecting, his legal right. It is not by accident that we use the same word in issuing both kinds of judgment: "A was right to C" and "A had a right to C." But since an account of the convergence of sense will only prove critical late in the book we will put off providing it here and make do with observing a few of the formal affinities between moral and legal "rights."

1) Claims about someone being morally right or having a right are character claims: they say, in the first case, that A was right to do C and, in the second case, that A was within his rights to do C.

2) As character claims, rights claims are truth claims. For any claim that 'A did C' to be true, it has to be accurate in three ways. It has to characterize C accurately, identify A accurately, and ascribe C to A accurately. Whether we chide Dee for coming late to a meeting, thank Bea for being helpful, admire Jay for raising an inconvenient truth, or charge you with armed robbery, we purport to characterize, identify,

and ascribe accurately. If our judgment mischaracterizes C, misidentifies A, or incorrectly ascribes C to A, then it fails to tell the truth.

3) "Right" judgments are either/or assertions. A was right in doing C or he was not. A had a right to do C or he did not.

4) A being right in doing C and A having the right to do C are both positive value judgments.

5) In judging that A was right to C or that A had a right to C we make the same value judgment about both A and C. If I praise A for C, C was the right thing to do and A was right in doing it, and if I blame A for C, C was the wrong thing to have done and A was wrong in doing it. And if A had a right to do C, then C was alright for A to do, and if C was alright for A to do then A was within his rights to do it.

Formal similarities are not always instructive but these are worth considering because of the root sensibility they share. If we are not mistaken in thinking that we can read a basis for both "right" and "rights" out of what it means for somebody to be resolved in good faith, we should be able to make better sense of the long-disputed connection between law and morality. Historically a great many influential thinkers have insisted that the law gets its legitimacy from a higher authority. For Augustine that legitimacy came from its accordance with God's law, for Natural Law philosophers from its accordance with the purposes of nature's laws, and for Thomas Jefferson's generation from what is implicit in being "human."

But being able to draw a coherent conceptual connection between legal rights and a higher authority of some sort turns out to be elusive, particularly now that the conceptual underpinnings of universal rights have rusted away. Today, few people would contend in philosophical seriousness that we "are endowed by our Creator with certain inalienable rights." Even Jefferson's older contemporary Edmund Burke called the "Rights of Man" an abstraction and not many decades later Jeremy Bentham referred to it as "nonsense upon stilts." When people pay lip-service to "human rights" today their lips are likely to curl a bit in irony.

The way out of this conceptual bind requires us to back away from trying to derive universal rights from what it is to be "natural" or "human" and derive them instead from what it means to be "personal," from what it means to be the character of someone's resolve. Since purporting to be a character of resolve involves purporting to optimize one's active moment in projecting one's life the way one does, to be a person is to assert the right to be a resolute being in good faith. Accordingly, to recognize someone as a person is to respect his right to project the greatest momentary being he can.

As a statement of our fundamental personal right, this raises some red flags, to be sure. We do not, after all, allow people to exploit one another on the grounds that they think they can actualize the greatest moment thereby. If we did we would be living in the kind of world Nietzsche envisioned, one in which it is acceptable for people to act without regard for the well-being of others.

If the red flags are to come down, we will have to find rational grounds for believing that it is inconceivable for a person to actualize himself most momentously by exploiting others. In chapter 5 we will explore this belief as the axiom of moral integrity. In the last chapter, we will see that a great deal rides on whether we have grounds for believing it. For now, we need only acknowledge that many of the inferences we will be discussing in this chapter depend on the plausibility of this belief.

When people raise rights issues they usually do so in the wake of some interaction that went bad. So we might best start by observing what is distinctive about the ones that don't go bad, the healthy ones, the ones in the context of which both parties actualize themselves most momentously in carrying their intentions through. What alone can guarantee that an interaction will be healthy is that the parties both have the right to interact and the right not to interact, the right to engage in and the right to disengage from any interaction. Only then can both be guaranteed the conditions for acting in good faith, which is the condition for being a person. That means one has the right to initiate any interaction that promises to increase one's moment and one has the right to turn down (or disengage from) any interaction that does not promise (or no longer promises) to do that.

We will call the former right *positive* because it involves *posing* an interactive course to another—be it to exchange greetings, share a taxi, co-sign a lease, pass a merry moment, or get married—and we will call the latter right *absolute* both because it *ab-solves* one from an interaction and because it always takes precedence over another's positive right: Bea invites Dee to a party. Bea has a positive right to extend the invitation and Dee has the absolute right to turn her down. Bea has no right to insist that Dee come to her party if Dee thinks that she'd get more satisfaction spending the evening at home.

An important thing to notice about positive and absolute personal rights is that they are reasonably claimed only relative to other personal rights holders. Bea couldn't be said to "invite" Dee to the party unless Dee could exercise the right to turn her down, nor for that matter would it make sense for Dee to turn Bea down in the absence of an invitation. The assertion of either a positive or absolute personal right assumes an interactive other who can also assert those rights.

Finally, there is a proviso attached to granting someone an absolute right if the interaction is already underway: he must make good on any damages that will result from his breaking it off. When somebody backs out of an ongoing interactive relationship he is likely to cause damage to the other interactor in the form of a loss of active moment. After all, parties to any interaction trust each other to see a course through (unless it becomes personally defeating to do so). Trusting an interactive partner—whether the interactive relationship is long-term and intimate or short-term and superficial—represents the interactors' mutual commitment to actualize their intentional lives together (again, unless or until doing so would mean one had to act in bad faith). So, whether it involves a business contract or a date to the County Fair, if A absolves from B, some of B's appointed satisfactions are likely to go disappointed with the result that B suffers a momentary loss of actual being. In line with our (still to be justified) insistence that all rightful interactions must respect both parties' right to greatest actualization, this implies that B can only absolve from A rightfully (that is, in a non-exploiting way) if he redresses A's loss.

We can summarize these ground rules for reasoning about people's rights: *(1) one can only assert a positive right relative to interactors with absolute rights, (2) absolute rights take precedence over positive ones, and (3) one can claim an absolute right only on personal grounds and only if he pays for whatever damage the absolution causes.*

It is time now to see whether these general entailments of treating others as characters of resolve really do underwrite our inferences about rights in practice. To make sure we sample widely, let us divide the field not only between positive and absolute rights claims but also between impersonal and personal interactions.

Rights Claims in Impersonal Interactions.

Earlier we found it useful to make our way into the subject of active presence by describing the form it takes in people who do not know one another personally. We saw that on the impersonal level each party's characterization of what the other is doing need only be rich enough to grasp the intention of his moves in their shared enterprise. One party has no need to be aware of how the other is trying to resolve his life. We found that by looking first at our experience of impersonal presence we were in a better position to account for what is distinctive about personal presence. We will follow the same strategy here, and for comparable reasons.

One way to draw the distinction between personal and impersonal interactions is in terms of the accountability the parties take on. In healthy impersonal interactions the parties share the commitment to bring about something they each intend for his own reasons.

You take your car into Kwicky's Car Care for an oil change. Kwicky greets you and you ask him whether he can do the job while you wait. He assures you that he can and tells you that he'll get to it in just a few minutes. Sure enough, forty-five minutes later he hands you the keys, you pay him, say goodbye, and drive off.

If you and Kwicky had been asked to project the course you expected your interaction to take you would do so in much the same way. Not only would you both envision much the same outcome but you would share expectations with respect to the kinds of moves each party would make leading up to that outcome. And even though each of you would characterize your interaction from his own perspective—he by saying he was changing somebody's oil and you by saying you were getting your oil changed—you would both expect to play your roles comfortably. You would both envision your common arrival at an agreed-upon resolution of your actions whereupon you would both regard the transaction as having been completed and its moment past.

It is reasonable to represent such an interactive agreement as a shared narrative. Granted, neither you nor Kwicky would have felt the need to tell a story—your transaction was too routinized for that—but if you had been pressed to do so you could have come up with a series of character claims (expressing mutual expectations) that would advance in coordination toward the outcome you both intended. That series—episodic moves finding a prescribed resolution—would play out formally much the way a conventional story plays itself out.

But, since rights issues do not typically arise when interactions go according to script, we need to complicate our illustration to focus on those issues. Suppose, for example, that you ask Kwicky whether he'll change the oil while you wait and he tells you that it'll be about an hour before he can get to it. You're disappointed (*dis-appointed* from the interactive course you'd invited him into). You have lots to do this morning so the thought of spending two hours watching TV game shows in Kwicky's waiting room is frustrating. You have two options: you can submit to the narrative he offers for your interaction or you can absolve from it. Upon deliberation you might decide that signing onto his projection of the course of interaction (i.e., submitting to his two-hour narrative) will save you time and trouble in the long run. On the other hand, you might conclude that there would be greater satisfaction on your part if you were to put off the oil change.

If you decide to back away from Kwicky's proposal, there is no question of your right to do so. You can say "no thanks," exchange pleasantries, and drive off. Kwicky would have preferred that you accept his terms because it would have added to his income—read: the moment of his agency would have been expanded by his increased purchasing power—but he could hardly challenge your right to leave, given the extra time he requested. He would assume that your absolute right trumped his positive one just as earlier we acknowledged that his absolute right trumped your request to get the job done in under an hour.

We noted earlier that the domain of interaction wherein positive and absolute rights claims have legitimacy is one in which the parties interacting are in a position to exercise the same rights, rights required if they are to form personal resolve in good faith. Now we're going to look at two cases where one party exercises a positive right to initiate an interaction but where questions can be raised as to whether the other party can exercise the correlative absolute right. Both of these cases concern the kind of television ads a person-respecting society should and should not allow.

It is common to think of TV ads as one-way communications, as stimuli that elicit a response. As useful as that way of looking at these ads may be, it overlooks a crucial feature many of them display. Advertisements are, in our analysis, interactive. The interaction takes place between the ad and the imagination of the potential consumer. The intention of the advertiser is obviously to induce potential consumers to become actual consumers. The goal of consumers is to live the richest and fullest life possible. The work of the ad, then, is to get consumers to imagine themselves living that richer, fuller life by consuming the product, and, in effect, coming to share the advertiser's intention.

Because TV ads exhibit interactivity in that sense, it would pay to look at them with interactive rights in mind to see how an advertiser's positive right to try to engage the viewer can violate a viewer's personal right to act in good faith.

Both of the examples we are about to consider involve what in some sense is "deceptive" advertising. In the founding sense of the term, deceptive ads snare the viewer—the "cieve" part of "deceive" means "to take, as in a trap." They trap him by preventing him from acting in his best interest, which well might be, to absolve from the intention the ad invites us to share.

A classic case of deceptive advertising would be one that misrepresents what the product is designed to do, what it costs, or how big it is. That would clearly undermine a viewer's ability to make the right consumer decision, the decision that would optimize his agency. In these classic cases, what counts as deceptive is reasonably clear. It is a factual distortion working to snare viewers and prevent them from making a decision that will optimize their life prospects.

There is another sort of deceptive ad that we not only tolerate but often enjoy watching. Why we permit such ads, it turns out, is difficult to state if we use the reasoning that governs the classic cases. Consider, for instance, the kind of ads whose narrative of consumption purports to resolve certain of the target viewers' life-orienting and momentous intentions. It may engage us with images of a mother succeeding at being a better mom to her kids by taking them out for fast food, or it may show us a husband in a loveless marriage rekindling the fire by taking his wife on a cruise. What is distinctive about these ads is that they don't simply try to get the targeted viewer to intend to consume the product; they try to make that intention important in the way he resolves his life.

In the basic sense of the term, people are often deceived by such ads. Yet we don't think of this sort of deception as culpable. Why not?

The traditional standard for deception is bequeathed to us by English Common Law. It is the "reasonable person" standard. Advertising is only deceptive when it deceives (to his detriment) a reasonable person. Reasonable" is of course a vague term, as everyone appreciates, but it is also an ambiguous one, which not everyone appreciates. Someone can be reasonable or unreasonable in terms of either category logic or character logic. With respect to the former, he might have mastered the basic principles governing categorical syllogisms. But that is no guarantee that his actions are reasonable by the standards of character logic. Actions are personally reasonable only when the actor determines their character in accord with the way he resolves his life. In that sense, his resolve (and any of its ingredient projects) is reasonable if, after deliberation, he finds that it (and they) promise to advance his greatest intentional satisfaction, that being his *raison d'etre* as a multi-intentioned agent.

When we naively assume that the coin of reasoning about action should always be denominated in the currency of categories, we muddle what common law means by "reasonable" and therefore what it means by "deceptive." A better way to make sense of being culpably deceived is to ask whether the deceived viewer was acting rationally in the personal sense when he resolved his life in the way the ad suggested he should.

Imagine that Mr. Gray, a middle-aged middle-manager, sees an ad for a sports car that promises to make him feel like a kid again. He buys the car with great anticipation only to find his rejuvenation petering out before the first oil change. In one last attempt to satisfy his quest for renewal, he demonstrates to some neighborhood teens how to drag race but smashes into a police car and breaks his leg instead.

Was the ad that inspired Mr. Gray deceptive in a way that should draw the attention of the Federal Trade Commission? According to common law it is actionably deceptive only if Mr. Gray was deceived as a reasonable person. Was he? Given his position as a successful business functionary we can assume that he was rational in the sense of being sufficiently adept at handling the real world. But can we also be confident that he was acting deliberatively in accord with his personal resolve? Apparently not. Gray would seem to have been rational in how he handled the categories of reality but irrational personally. His failure was not in thinking unrealistically; it was in not self-actualizing in good faith when he resolved to consume as he did. What Gray got wrong was not *factually* wrong but *actually* wrong.

Our intuitive reliance on the "reasonable person" standard, it would seem, trades as much on its personal sense as on the sense consistent with category logic. What this example illustrates, then, is an instance in which we readily use character logic to draw reasonable conclusions about a certain kind of deceptive advertising.

Our second illustration is also one that calls for character logic to determine, but in this case our intuitive defense of the rights at stake gets ignored by an insistence on using only category claims in our reasoning. We are thinking here about advertisements directed at children.

We know that children are for the most part incapable of judging what is in their best interests. That makes them ripe for exploitation unless we protect them. Advertising to children, therefore, can easily become problematic. The ad industry presupposes that no harm will come to children if we adopt appropriate safeguards concerning the kinds of product being pushed. If the product doesn't do the child any tangible harm, the assumption is that an ad that convinces a child to use or consume it can't do him any harm either.

But here's the flaw in that reasoning: the harm or damage it considers is only that which can be identified by the usual scientific means. That leaves out of consideration harm to the active life of the child, now and in the future. Obviously, tangible harm is easier to detect. Selling lead-painted toys or clothes with buttons that can be swallowed falls into that category. But actual harm—the damage to the child as an emerging person—can be insidious too. It can foreclose on a child's future active possibilities. The two kinds of damage often overlap, to be sure—if lead paint damages my innards it will no doubt damage my active prospects as well. Personal damage, by contrast, may not show up physiologically, and it can work to defeat the person the child will become even in the absence of what is immediately perceptible as harm.

We have already seen how fundamentally a child's narrative imagination figures in constructing the unified intentional life toward which he advances.

We have seen how important it is for him to learn to negotiate a narrative environment that presents resolutions germane to his own ability to characterize his action. Seen against this developmental need, ads can be seen to pose impediments for children who grow up in environments saturated with them. Since every narrative an ad presents gets resolved in consumption, that saturation poses the danger that by crowding out other sorts of narrative and relentlessly inviting children to organize their still fragile intentional lives around acts of consumption, a child's bid for individuality is likely to be brought up short. The child is likely to experience a delay in entering adolescence. Worse still, he may never, during adolescence or afterward, be able to look beyond patterns of consumption for the available ingredients of personal resolution. That impoverished diet for imagined possibilities fosters a life of highly constrained momentary being. Since its moments of movement are largely contained in moments of consuming, it proposes little meaning beyond sustaining those patterns, in which case it would also be impoverishing in the interactive and historical registers a child must develop as well.

A person-fostering society, we would argue, has actual grounds for banning advertising to children even if no real grounds are apparent. By making more room in their narrative environment for more momentously active imaginative projects, we better initiate children into more momentous lives, which is of course the aim of person-fostering. This case suggests that the logic of scientific reasoning is restrictive in the sense that it obfuscates alternatives to organizing one's life around consumption.

We have been looking at two modes of interaction in which one party's assertion of a positive right is wrongfully claimed against people who cannot exercise a right to absolve, either because their capacity to do so has been undermined (in the case of culpably deceptive ads) or because it has not yet developed (in the case of ads to children). Now we turn to the other category of rights violations, those that occur when one party absolves from an interaction without compensating the other party for damages suffered.

We have represented personal damage as momentary depletion, and we should not let the expediency of reckoning it in monetary terms hide the momentary measure at its base. After a major disappointment, like a break-up or the loss of a job, people don't just *feel* deflated, brought down, or depressed; they are aware of *being* that way. Since money is purchasing power and can be said to purchase momentary satisfaction, there is some logic to paying for this loss in cash.

But active awareness, that is, awareness of what we are doing, is largely tacit, so it may be impossible to justify any specific monetary equivalent to the loss of personal moment. But because the moment of someone's personal projection of intentional movement has volume, the personal cost of any absolution is determined in principle by the moments of resolute movement lost because of it.

To illustrate how someone's awareness of relative momentary depletion might register in an assessment of momentary damages we will consider first some impersonal cases in which little damage is involved and then at some cases where more serious personal capital is at stake.

You've reluctantly chosen to go ahead with the oil change at Kwicky's, but after an hour of sulking in his waiting room you get a call from a friend who advises you that your car is about to be repossessed. You're short on cash, and suddenly the oil change is worthless and a drain on your meager resources.

You and Kwicky had entered into a commercial interaction intending to see it through, and each of you was vested in its outcome. Each of you—you by waiting and watching, Kwicky by driving your car around and hoisting it overhead—stood to gain if the other did his part and stood to lose if he did not. Your mutual understanding made you parties to a joint venture, one that you expected would satisfy you both. But now you want out. You explain the situation and Kwicky (righteous guy that he is) sympathizes with your need to back out of the deal. Accordingly, he takes the car down from the rack, and you ask, "How much do I owe you?" You are obliged to ask that because you know he is within his rights to charge you "for his time." If he had the car up on the lift but hadn't yet pulled the drain-plug his loss would work out to the usual labor cost prorated by the short time he spent on it. Something along those lines would set reasonable terms for your absolution and seem fair to you both.

When business deals are more complex, the parties are likely to draw up a formal contract in which they explicitly agree how each can be expected to act in the interactive project they are committing to undertake. We usually think of contracts as explicit agreements written by attorneys and signed by the parties to them. But some of them are only oral agreements, and some are altogether non-verbal. So it is bound to be an issue occasionally whether something somebody calls a contract is actionable. And that means it is crucial for us to share an understanding of what it takes for an agreement to be contractual.

We start with the assumption that a contract constitutes an interaction of some sort. That may seem more obviously true than our earlier insistence that we look at TV commercials as interactions. To do that, we had to focus on the viewers' part in the interaction as an act of imagination, one in which he incorporates the consumption of the product as an element in his personal narrative.

This may have seemed a bit of a conceptual stretch, but a look at what makes a contract binding shows us that a comparable solitary act of resolve on the part of one party can prove sufficient for its legitimacy. We can see this when we consider the provocative ring to Charles Fried's contention that a contract is simply a promise.[15] This is an intriguing proposal because we all understand what it is to promise someone something, so if contracts are simply promises we should have no problem recognizing them. Yet traditionally, a contract is taken to be an interactive *quid pro quo*. Promises don't seem to require that kind of reciprocity. So, since defining a contract as a promise ignores the reciprocity we associate with contractual relations, it cannot, some argue, be simply a promise. Fried's critics have insisted that if A promises something to B, A's promise is only a contract if B is obliged to do something in return, something tangible that we can regard as a "consideration."

Fried rebuts this line of criticism by citing a precedent-setting case[16] where a promise without any apparent consideration provided by the promisee was validated as a contract in court. The case concerned an uncle who promised to pay his nephew $5000 on his twenty-first birthday if he, the nephew, refrained from smoking or drinking until that day. The nephew complied, but the uncle's executor refused to pay him because, he claimed, the promise had been made without consideration and was thus not a contract. Fried acknowledges that "[it] is a standard textbook proposition that in Anglo-American law a promise is not binding without consideration," [17] and he admits that it is entirely possible that the nephew's forbearance amounted to nothing tangible (perhaps he found tobacco and alcohol disgusting and was never tempted). Yet the court found in favor of the nephew: "[Having] fully performed the conditions imposed, it is of no moment whether such performance actually proved a benefit to the promiser" (*Hamer v. Sidway*). Of course, whether that argument convinces us depends upon whether we regard the court's decision as the right one, but if we do (and we do) then Fried thinks we must admit that promises are, after all, contractually binding even without corresponding considerations.

The light to be shed on this dispute comes when we remind ourselves that contracts represent interactions between characters of resolve. This is important because it shows us how a promisee's moves in response to a promise can constitute a consideration without being tangible. In the case of the nephew, we would expect him to project his life story going forward different-

---

[15] Charles Fried, *Contract as Promise* (Cambridge, Massachusetts and London, England: Harvard University Press, 1981).
[16] Hamer v. Sidway (New York Court of Appeals, 1891)
[17] Fried, p 28.

ly as a result of the bequest. Upon hearing his uncle's promise he may well have rethought his future in light of its new possibilities ($5000 in 1891 amounted to well over $100,000 in today's money.) In the light of his uncle's promise during the months before his big birthday celebration, he might have hobnobbed at the country club (or its 19th-century equivalent) rather than socialize at the local saloon the way he used to. Perhaps he went into debt buying clothes at a fancy emporium instead of making do with the rougher weaves he was used to. Based on the prospect of that nest egg, he may have passed up a dreary but well-paying job in favor of a more creative though less lucrative one. Since it is reasonable to assume that at least some elements of his resolute project had his uncle's bequest as their condition, at least some of the satisfactions he projected depended on that promise being kept.

Does such an adjustment to his resolve count as interactive reciprocity? It seems reasonable to read it that way since he took up the course of action proffered by his uncle, altering his projection of action to share in his uncle's intended narrative of sobriety, expectation, and reward. That narrative resolved itself in the bequest they both intended. The uncle's executor had to honor that outcome simply because the nephew had "counted on it."

The Heightened Moment of Civil Disobedience

In a person-respecting society we design laws to foster healthy ways of interacting. We do that for the practical reason that laws give our impersonal relations predictability, which in turn enables us to coordinate our own lives to greater moment. So when someone breaks the law he in effect absolves from an interactive arrangement people count on. Lawbreaking tends thereby to diminish personal satisfaction in society.

But against our general arrangement for dealing with betrayers of the social order, one class of law-breaking cuts a distinctive figure. In cases of what we recognize as civil disobedience, we forebear condemning act and actor alike on the grounds that such acts are justified by a higher authority. Pressed to define what that higher authority is, however, we find ourselves at a collective loss. When we think of people we'd put in that category—people like Thoreau, Gandhi, Rosa Parks, Martin Luther King, or Ken Saro-Wiwa—we find that they shared no common language of justification. Gandhi in drawing salt from the sea might have cited *Satyagraha*, resistance through non-violence. Rosa Parks, when she sat in the front of the bus, probably felt justified by her sense of dignity as well as her tired feet. King was committed to the power of loving one's enemies as a way to realize social change. The diversity in the appeals they made yields no formula for justifying some small class of law-breaking.

The view said to be most widely treated as orthodox tries to meet this challenge by withholding judgments about the reasonableness of their various appeals[18] in favor of directing our attention to the "conscientiousness" of the actors, to the fact that they *thought* they were doing the right thing. One could of course object that this opens the door to suicide bombers and abortion-doctor killers, but if one assumes the axiom of moral integrity (as we do provisionally, pending our discussion of it in chapter 5) such people are disqualified from counting as civilly disobedient.

But even if we insist that the civilly disobedient person be non-exploitatively conscientious, that state of mind by itself isn't sufficient to qualify him as civilly disobedient. It is possible to imagine that Dee, when she drives back home late at night, often turns left on the red light a block from her home and that she does so with a clear conscience since she can see clearly that no cars are coming toward the intersection from any direction. She may be behaving conscientiously but hers is not an act of civil disobedience, nor would we try to justify it with an appeal to a higher authority.

What seems more decisive in governing our intuitions in the matter is our sense of a law-breaker's absolute personal right. Whether a law-breaker is civilly disobedient is a matter of whether he can claim an absolute personal right to break the law. He, as well as any other person, has the right to absolve from any law if and only if he could not live in good faith if he did not. With Martin Luther he says, "Here I stand; I can do no other." If we picture Gandhi buying his salt like everybody else or a weary Rosa Parks standing in the back of the bus, we find ourselves picturing a defeated person. Complying with British demands would have compromised Gandhi by undoing the very quality of resolve that made him "Mahatma." Ministering in accordance with the racial narratives of the Old South would have cost King his momentous movement in the achievement of social justice for African-Americans. Submitting to Nigeria's and Shell Oil's narrative for his Ogoni homeland would have defeated Ken Saro-Wiwa personally more than the hangman's noose.

These people differed from all the others for whom complying with the law meant making the best of a bad situation. Perhaps they weighed the cost of resistance and found it too high; perhaps they lacked the imagination even to do that. But, for those rare individuals who inhabit a sufficiently extensive character of interactive accomplishment with a sufficiently extensive historical importance, complying with the law would be self-diminishing. It would degrade them communally and/or historically more than the punishment

---

[18] Gene G. James, "The Orthodox Theory of Civil Disobedience," Social Theory and Practice, Vol. 2. No. 4 (Fall 1973), p. 490.

they accept degrades their immediate activity. In breaking the law they are actualizing themselves to the fullest, which we recognize as every person's right. It is because we see them as such persons that we find them justified in breaking the law. Their higher righteousness is grounded in their right to absolve on personal grounds.

Ironically, the only true test for the legitimacy of someone's claim to absolve on personal grounds is his willingness to accept the sanctions attached to breaking the law. A willingness to submit to the state's penalty is the only thing that can supply evidence for the law-breaker's good faith; it is only by submitting the substantial deactivation of his individual life that he can show that the interactive and historical importance of his illegal action outweighs whatever loss of moment his body's confinement or even death occasions.

Rights assertions between personal partners

The difference between interacting on a personal and an impersonal level is marked in some European languages by distinct pronouns of address. When Germans address some people with *Du* and others with *Sie* they seem to be observing what has as its intuitive source the personal/impersonal fault line we have been surveying. *Du* appropriately addresses those whose resolve one is committed to actualizing fully, like family members and friends. *Du* also addresses members of one's church (since church membership is understood to confederate members into a single character of resolve: the will of God) and children (whose agency for now is largely determined by the resolve of those who interact with them). *Sie* is appropriate when an interaction is accountable only to the role each party plays.

What makes this distinction interactively indispensable is that if the parties don't classify their involvement the same way they may well suffer a confusion of expectations. We are more accountable to those in personal partnerships in that we owe it to our partner to live by the requirements of both of our projects. Our impersonal interactors, by contrast, expect only that we move in accord with the immediate aim of our interaction.

Calling a relationship personal makes it more *important* in that it *imports* greater moment into the interactive presence of both parties. That tends to put more at stake when one party breaks off a relationship, yet the rules to determine their rights are the same: the only ground a party has for absolving rightfully is that his good faith requires it, and then only if he makes up for any loss of moment suffered by his partner.

One place to see this paradigm illustrated with cartoon clarity is in the stock TV situation comedies that are driven by spats that temporarily fray a relationship between friends or spouses. They are gestures toward personal absolution, not genuine breaks; still, they can be read as bearing the form of a righteous absolution. Bea and Jay argue, and Bea momentarily does something that undermines Jay's intentions. She borrows his car without telling him and then dents a fender. He is furious.

Now their relationship has temporarily disintegrated. But, of course, the show being a comedy, we know they'll be reconciled in the end. Notice though what has to happen for that happy ending to be possible. The contretemps must be negotiated in an almost ritualistic sequence of movements toward reconciliation. Bea must acknowledge the damage she did, she must repair the damage, and she must modify her resolve to better accord with Jay's good faith requirements. When those steps have been taken the partnership will be back up and running.

The first move is usually marked with the words, "I'm sorry." To be "sorry" is to be "sore, pained and sensitive," but not with one's own injury. When Bea says she is sorry she is saying she is sore with Jay's hurt. And to be sore with the other's hurt is to position oneself back into the resolve where the hurt is, where the damage was done. "I'm sorry I hurt you," says Bea. By declaring herself sore with Jay's hurt, Bea declares herself once again resolutely *with* Jay, no longer absolved from him.

But Bea's saying "I'm sorry" is not enough to make things right. She must make good on the damage. She must "make it up to him." To make up is to move in two ways, first in her imagination: to "make up" is to think up, like when one makes up an excuse. What needs making up is an iteration of their partnership that better accommodates the resolve of both of them. Second, she must "make up" for the loss Jay suffered. That might involve promising to pay Kwicky's bill for the car's bodywork. But Jay too may have to examine certain extenuating circumstances that prompted her behavior, circumstances that he bears some responsibility for. Maybe he'll offer to share in the repair costs. That will seal the reconciliation.

Of course, when an absolution from a personal relationship is permanent, the damage is likely to be greater. How much greater depends on how momentous the relationship was. On the low end of that continuum are friendships sustained by convenience. We can imagine that our senator, now fully resolved to run for president, is a casual friend of a Hollywood mogul. They are personal friends in a minimal way in that each knows roughly how the other fits his or her life together and each (for the time being) honors the requirements of that composition so far as he or she is privy to it. The senator, eyeing her party's nomination for president, arranges to have lunch with the mogul, a man notorious for his salacious and repulsively violent movies. Her intention is to solicit a campaign contribution. His intention is to assure himself that she's not beholden to those canting moralists who'll make his life more difficult if she's elected. He thinks he has reason to expect she'll be open to policies that shield his business (that being his interest in "joining her campaign"), but he also knows that she can't afford to have their partnership develop into a campaign issue. For that reason he's pledged to delay the release of a particularly graphic film, so scandalous that he knows it will draw huge crowds, until after Election Day. By his reckoning, it will be worth the delay to have a friend in Washington. The senator isn't naive either. She knows his business, why he may support her, and what his expectations are, and she knows that he is aware of her need to protect her interests.

Though this is not an important personal relationship for either of them, some measure of moment would clearly be at stake were either to absolve from their understanding. The mogul's financial contribution to the senator amounts to a contribution to her agency, "extending the reach" of her campaign; the mogul's reach is enhanced in turn insofar as his resolve now influences how the senator will be disposed to vote on relevant legislation. Their relationship thus promises to extend the active moment of each, the senator with her new money becoming a greater political force and the mogul becoming a bigger player in the industry. But it is accepted by both that the character of their ongoing interaction is conditioned on its continued convenience to each. The senator respects the mogul's business interests and is disposed to accommodate them unless it threatens her political life to do so and, should his action ever threaten to counteract hers, she reserves the right to absolve from their arrangement. Comparably, the mogul is committed to supporting her for only as long as her positions on proposed legislation accommodate his interests. If his interests were to require him to absolve there would be nothing vindictive in his withdrawal of support, and she would respect his right to do so. Nor would he take it personally if she voted against his interests to avoid risking defeat for a second term. The senator won't jeopardize her career, and the mogul accepts that, nor will the mogul jeopardize his career and the senator accepts that.

Because both accept the contingent basis for their friendship and neither banks much on it, any damages caused by one party backing out would be slight. If the senator finds herself in a tight race with a lifestyle conservative and withdraws from their little understanding by voting against the mogul's interests, she would accept his withdrawal of financial support as reasonable and regard her depletion of projected resources a fair price to pay for her absolution. And if for some reason it suddenly became extremely lucrative for the mogul to release his edgy film before the election, he'd know she would feel betrayed and he could no longer count on her legislative restraint. The possible loss of that restraint is a price he might be willing to pay.

When we consider partnerships farther up the continuum of relational richness, we find them more comprehensive of the persons involved, hence more damaging when broken. Friendships all involve a commitment to honor both parties' resolve in how each projects his life. Even the friendship of convenience enjoyed by the mogul and the senator was predicated on such commitment despite the contingencies that made it fragile. But we need to keep in mind that no friendship or personal partnership of any kind can abrogate either party's right to absolve on personal grounds.

What makes deeper, more involving friendships less fragile is that a breakup would (unlike that between the senator and the mogul) occasion a depletion of moment in all three dimensions of the abandoned partner's being, in how richly intention-satisfying his life is, in how much of others' lives his resolve now creates moment, and in how much historical importance he attaches to what they are doing.

Deliberating the termination of a deeply involving relationship is always wrenching. The cost of splitting up can sometimes seem so personally shattering that one is immobilized. That seems to be what is happening when abused women cling to abusive relationships. Those who want to help them are sometimes tempted to think that they fail to *understand* their situation clearly. Surely any objective third party would find separation the obvious choice, they reason, so there must be a cognitive problem preventing her from seeing the situation for what it is.

This diagnosis is problematic though, not only because it plays to the stereotype of women being prone to irrationality but because it mis-focuses what it is she fails to grasp. What she cannot conceive of is a course of action going forward wherein she absolves from her abuser and lives a more satisfying life. If no such alternative narrative possibility opens up to her, then her refusal to absolve is her only rational choice as she perceives it.

In the case of an abused spouse, there is no question of her right to sue for divorce. Anyone being exploited and harmed in a relationship has, transparently, a fundamental personal right to cut free of it. But what about cases in which there is no exploitation? How do we define a rightful divorce in them?

In our present cultural climate, our respect for every person's absolute rights leads us to allow any marital partner to get a divorce when, after careful deliberation, he finds himself genuinely unable to actualize himself best in the relationship, conditional on his recompensing his former spouse for damages suffered.

Our societal leniency in justifying divorce is thought by some to challenge the distinctiveness of marriage among personal partnerships. We regard ourselves as free to dissolve friendships without much ceremony or sanction. If

Kay, with a great job offer in hand, moved away from the town where her friend Em lived, and if she did so with no more ceremony than a goodbye party and friendly hug, and if thereafter she lost touch with her old friend, we would hardly assume that what she did was immoral or illegal. We don't socially officiate over the breakup of non-marital partnerships. But if we grant any marital partner the right to break off the relationship, then the question imposes itself: on what basis do we socially regulate marriages? An answer to that question should help us draw up a social definition of marriage that will enable us to clarify its rights and responsibilities.

Not many decades ago most people assumed that it was always (or almost always) wrong to get a divorce. They thought of marriages as permanent partnerships, "until death do us part," and they justified impediments to dissolving them as ways to protect the family-rearing function thought to be (paradigmatically if not always actually) at the heart of the relationship's purpose. This understanding has come under attack from those who argue that the institution should be more broadly understood to accommodate couples for whom child-rearing is not what their relationship is about. Traditionalists fear that definitional tampering will open the door to any manner of relationship qualifying as a marriage (under a new definition), with the result that the institution will be weakened in ways that are not in society's interest.

Perhaps we can raise the question of society's person-respecting and person-fostering role in a more helpful way if we construe marriage as a partnership between two characters of resolve. That leads us to ask what formal features would qualify a partnership between characters of resolve such that society would be justified in regulating it. Presumably, a person-fostering society has an interest in privileging a form of partnership only if that form systematically actualizes persons more momentously than any other. If that is our bedrock political principle, then the traditionalist view of marriage could persuade us only if it is reasonable to believe that marriages so defined have a person-respecting, person-fostering advantage.

To see whether this is so we need to take into account all three dimensions of a person's momentary being, all three active sites where movement in the character of his resolve is actualized. We need to ask whether it is reasonable to believe that persons in traditional marriages hold the advantage in at least one of the three, that traditionally married people are either more fully resolved than other people, more interactively satisfied, or embarked on greater historical accomplishment. If traditional marriage is systematically advantageous by at least one of these criteria then (but only then) would it make sense for a society to set it apart from other partnerships for special legal and moral treatment. If it turns out that it is not systematically advantageous—that privileging traditional marriages cannot be supported on the grounds of being more person-fostering—then we must ask what kind of partnership, if any, does carry marital rights and responsibilities.

First, do we have reason for thinking that a traditionally married man or woman is likely to achieve more coherence in his or her intentional life? If there is reason to think that traditional marriage offers its parties a greater opportunity for inner resolution than other partnerships, or for that matter un-partnered lives, then the traditionalists win the argument. But it would be arbitrary to make that claim without evidence. Several philosophers, including Gabrielle Suchon and Simone de Beauvoir, have argued that traditional marriage does not deliver the same promise to husbands and wives. They contend that traditional marriage, at least from the perspective of women, is neither person-respecting nor person-enhancing.

It is certainly conceivable that somebody's non-traditional marriage could be as conducive to optimal internal resolution as a traditional one. It is conceivable as well that an unmarried person could achieve an admirable degree of personal coherence. Indeed, those putative paragons of inner serenity, the saints or holy people of various religious traditions, have tended to lead lives of chaste solitude.

As for the claim that traditionally married people are better enriched by each other's lives, that too seems arbitrary. Traditional marriages vary widely in how involved and co-dependent the partners are and also in how faithful they are.

That leaves the criterion of historical significance. It is here that defenders of traditional marriage usually make their stand. Few would deny that child-rearing gives a person's life greater historical importance. After all, a parent's resolve molds the intentions of a child so as to create moment in his future life. That extends both parents' actualization into the future. Hyperbolic though Plato's Socrates may have been when (in the *Symposium*) he invited us to think of child-rearing as a bid for immortality, he confirmed our intuition that parents are (as character logic permits us to say) momentously extended as characters of resolve into their children's continuing characters. Such an extension at least gestures in the direction of immortality.

But biological parenting only gestures in that direction, as Socrates admitted. Famously, in fact, he regarded dialogical partnerships as more ontologically significant in the progeny they produce. Whether or not one agrees with him, there seems to be no obvious reason to think of family-rearing as the most momentous accomplishment a marriage could undertake. There is nothing absurd in expecting marriages otherwise resolved to actualize great historical moment in other ways.

It does, however, provide a challenge to non-traditionalists. Traditional marriages in which children are successfully reared actualize moment into the future. The claim that they can accomplish this is one we can all attest to. For non-traditional marriages, by contrast, the kind of historical import that can be achieved resists being typed. Yet, that doesn't make it less arbitrary to insist that child-rearing is the only enduring legacy a marriage can achieve. Traditional marriages, then, have a compelling but not an exclusive claim to social value and the need for institutional protection.

This leads us to conclude that, while it is arbitrary to delimit marriage to its family-rearing function or to privilege that particular function above all others, it does seem reasonable to insist that marriage be a commitment to some life-extending projects, the importance of which surpasses in accomplishment the lives of its partners. Marriages must promise not only to accomplish their partners' lives optimally but also to open active possibilities for people whose lives they touch in ways that create momentary gain for future persons. The vows that are privileged and the formal social status institutionalized as marriage are meant to protect that legacy. If we think it through in terms of character logic, we can understand why traditional marriage has been deemed valuable and also how its critics can coherently argue that alternative forms of marriage can be just as valuable. If partnerships of whatever ilk function to create future personal value, they also merit the special treatment the institution of marriage has received.

Finally then, what shall we say about the right to absolve from a marriage, the right to divorce? Under what conditions should society grant a divorce? Until the adoption of no-fault divorce, it was only possible to dissolve a marriage if one party could be shown to have broken the vow culpably (by abandonment or adultery, for example). This meant one party had to be judged to be in the wrong. A wronged person, a person whose marriage had already been betrayed, could then be granted a divorce since the dissolution it marked had already taken place by the wrong-doing spouse's absolution. That way, society avoided putting asunder what God hath joined.

Now that a more intuitive approach has won out, an absolver can justify his act without blaming or accepting blame as long as he makes his case on personal grounds. The usual language cites "irreconcilable differences." The obvious question is how we know when a difference is irreconcilable in a sense that that justifies divorce. Character logic answers as follows: differences are irreconcilable when they represent incompatibilities that cannot be negotiated away in good faith. When one partner's life can only meet the requirements of the other's good faith by sacrificing the requirements of his own, the differences are irreconcilable in a way that justifies the dissolution of the marriage without either side having to accept blame.

As for the requirement of paying damages, the language we use to describe an absolution reflects this requirement. To absolve from a partnership means to "withdraw" from someone's life and that word connotes not only "to take back or away," but "to cause to decline, decrease, or disappear" (*OED*). The damages we assess in divorces are meant to redress lost moments not only to newly dissatisfied elements in the absolved-from partner's present intentional life but also to whatever shrinkage in his prospects he will suffer. If his partnership was comprehensive of a great deal of his life, he will likely be reduced in all three dimensions of his personal moment: reduced in the range of his individual projects now blocked from actualization, reduced by the sudden lack of productive interaction in his life, and reduced in historical significance that the marriage had sustained relationally. One could say that the great momentary damage done in a divorce is commensurate with the ontological wealth it represented when it was stable.

But the damages that must be paid when one party absolves from a marriage go beyond compensation for loss of moment in the future. We all know of cases in which either the husband or wife has incurred a disproportionate amount of the toil in the past under the implicit agreement that the extra sacrifice would be redeemed in the end. In terms of character logic, we can say that the partner who made the sacrifice was counting on the added moment that would eventually be shared by the marriage partners. For example (to continue the painful saga), imagine that in her early years of marriage Bea had given up her promising career as a concert violinist to raise a family while her husband Jay climbed the corporate ladder. Now that their children are grown, he finds that his significantly increased status adds to his appeal, especially to supermodel types less than half his age. Unable to resist the temptation, he implores Bea to accept that she has now become a hindrance in his further climb toward momentous personal distinction.

What are Bea's rights in this matter? For her, divorce would cost more than future prospects of the interactive life with Jay she believes she is entitled to. His absolving from their relationship would trivialize her past sacrifices. The momentum of her musical career having been definitively broken, it is reasonable for her to receive compensation for the losses she incurred in the past as well as for the diminished moment of a shattered future.

We have examined different kinds of interactive relations—from the impersonal to the personal and from the casually personal (the unvowed) to the intimately personal (including those formalized in marital vows)—with an eye to questions of rights and how we intuitively answer them. Our aim has been to see how respect for the positive and absolute rights determined by our being as characters of resolve governs how we reason in such cases, or, alternatively, how it accounts for our discomfort with reasoning not governed by it.

In at least the sample cases we have examined we seem intuitively to respect someone's positive right to initiate a healthy interaction on the condition that his invitation can be turned down on personal grounds or later absolved from on personal grounds. Those cases also bear out the claim that damage settlements reflect our sense of the loss of active moment suffered by the absolved-from party.

Chapter 4

Personal Responsibility

We have been discussing the fundamental personal rights someone must have in order to function as a character of resolve in good faith. Now we turn to the correlative question of personal responsibility, correlative because in making both rights judgments and responsibility judgments we are governed by our identification of a person as the present character of his resolve. Because a person *is* his individual character of resolve, he is responsible for all and only the actions that are ingredient in that resolve. That is how we make the binary judgment: whether or not A was responsible for C depends on whether or not A was resolved in doing C. But ascriptions of responsibility are also concerned with how blameworthy or praiseworthy A was for doing C. That quantitative judgment needs to be investigated. As we are going to see, how much praise or blame we assign depends on two factors, the momentary value, negative or positive, we assign to C and the momentary value we assign to A.

We begin with the binary matter. We noted earlier that when an 'A did C' claim identifies A as a person (as it does in forensic reasoning) the logical relationship between A as a character of resolute action and C as the character of the ascribed action is one of mutual implication. For A to be personally responsible for C the relationship between A's character-identity and C's significance as a character of action must be one of mutual implication. That makes sense because (1) when C is done resolutely (as it must be if it is to be ascribed to A personally) C has its fullness of meaning in A's story and (2) A as he is identified in his story includes C. We can hear ourselves acknowledging this mutual implication when we insist that for A to be guilty of crime C he must be *implicated* in C, he must be *folded into* it. A can be identified when C unfolds its greater active significance narratively. Of course, in A's awareness of doing C, the narrative that identifies A is only tacitly present. But that is enough to make A and C mutually implicative in the context of A's story. C properly understood in the storied context of A's resolve is what identifies A as a person if and only if the character of resolve that identifies A includes C. The person and his act thus have their being in one another's character.

This is born out by what we assume about A's awareness in doing C when we hold him responsible for C. We assume that he was aware of C both as a discrete act and as an element of his resolve. A's active awareness, one might say, is the conceptual hinge enabling us to connect A with C. Just as the middle term connects S and P in a way that justifies drawing the conclusion of a categorical syllogism, A's active awareness connects A and C in a way that justifies holding A responsible.

To see how our intuitive understanding of personal responsibility depends upon the mutual implication between the character of the act and the character of the actor, and then to see how that equivalence determines the quantity of praise or blame we ascribe, we must first examine A's active awareness as it links itself logically to both A and C. For A to be personally responsible for C, A's active awareness must imply and be implied by both A and C. The necessary connection between A's active awareness and C is clear enough. We observed earlier that A couldn't be judged as having stolen a suitcase if the evidence showed that he *thought* he was taking his own suitcase. Similarly, meaning to tell someone the truth but getting it wrong wouldn't count as lying nor would blundering into the wrong apartment count as burglary. If we charge A with C, we have to assume that A's active awareness qualifies C as action of the type that is appropriate for that charge.

The other required implication—that A's active awareness is an indication of who he is—has posed more of a philosophical challenge. We cannot get along without assuming the connection in practice: as George Fletcher points out, the "distinguishing feature of excusing conditions is that they preclude an inference from the act to the actor's character."[19] In terms of character logic, this means that the binary judgment—that A is or is not personally responsible for C—depends upon both connections being intact. There must be a connection between A's active awareness and the character of his resolve and between his active awareness and the specific action he is being charged with.

The other kind of judgment implicit in responsibility ascriptions is quantitative: how blame/praiseworthy is A for C? When A is "charged" with C, the charge represents "a material load; that which can be borne, carried or received" (OED). But whether a particular load is reasonable for the guilty-as-charged person to bear depends both on how big the load is and how big the person is. We can give formal specificity to this dual variability by recalling that both A's active awareness of C and A's active awareness of being A in doing C can be said to have momentary value. If we blame A for C, it means that we think that, in doing C, A de-actualized someone's momentary being,

---

[19]George Fletcher, *Rethinking Criminal Law.* Little Brown and Company (Boston, 1978), pp. 799-800.

robbed him of his ability to satisfy his intentions. In that case, C registers with negative momentary value. But A too has momentary value: resolve is comprehensive by degree over someone's intentional life. So it makes sense to speak of somebody's personal life as determined in volume; some people lead more momentous lives than others. Their course comprehends more intentional movement.

That makes the volume of moment in A's active awareness in doing C the product of both A's moment and C's. Given the mutual implication of an act's character and its actor's character in ascriptions of personal responsibility, it follows that the degree of A's blameworthiness for C is determined by the product of A's positive volume of moment and C's negative volume. How praiseworthy A is for C is the product of A's positive volume and C's positive value. The more momentous A is and the more momentous C is, the more praise or blame we impose on A.

To show how this formula works in practice, let us look at several ways people can be held responsible for their actions by distinguishing the several ways A can be formally related to C. 1) C can be resolved in A's personal story to a degree that is fully comprehensive of her intentional life (recall, we are using feminine pronouns gender-inclusively but distinctively to designate persons—if such there be—who are *fully integrated* in their intentional being). In this case A would be *fully* responsible for C. 2) C can be resolved in A's personal story, but that story is only partially comprehensive of A's intentional life. In this case A would be responsible for C but in a *diminished* way. 3) C can be A's irresolute action, in which case A can be judged to have acted *irresponsibly* in doing C. 4) A may be a character of resolve no longer narratively coherent with C, in which case it would be right to *forgive* A. 5) A may no longer have a personal story, in which case A would not be personally responsible for C even in a diminished way.

A is resolved in C: A is fully responsible for C

For A to be fully responsible for C, A must not only be resolved in the accomplishment of C but wholly integrated in that moment. Only then could her active awareness bear the whole of her agency. We can think of this in terms of her personal presence. Being wholly resolved in the accomplishing of C, A would be fully present in the moment of C. Being wholly at one with what she did, we would have no basis for mitigating her responsibility. (Keep an open mind, if you will, about whether there are or could be such fully resolved persons in this formal sense. We will deal with that issue in chapter 5.)

Think for example of why we heap surpassing praise on those we honor for their civil disobedience. We honor not just the great things they did but the great integrity they seemed to bear in doing them. That is why people who want to undermine a "movement" try to poke holes in the character of its leader. And that is why those who seek a carte blanche in dealing with a Hitler, Stalin, or Osama bin Laden do so by demonizing them, making them wholly evil persons so that any measures taken against them can be justified.

A is partially resolved in C: A is diminished in his responsibility for C

Purity of heart, said Kierkegaard, is to will one thing. But who among us is pure? Though we might seek single-mindedness for the sake of greater intentional satisfaction, few (if any) of us, multi-intentioned agents that we are, succeed in coordinating our lives fully. Most of us intend unresolved and sometimes unresolvable satisfactions, half expecting to accomplish some task, say, passing a midterm examination in organic chemistry without having done the work that would make such success likely. William James wrote that

> [e]very one knows cases of this incomplete and ineffective desire for reform,—drunkards whom, with all their self-reproaches and resolves, one perceives to be quite unwilling seriously to contemplate *never* being drunk again![20]

Resolutions to reform one's life, especially when they require that we break longstanding habits, as James' example suggests, are notoriously difficult to optimize.

It is not uncommon to harbor these un-integrated intentions by wishful thinking. Some people bank on winning the lottery. Others hope to be "discovered" like Hollywood stars of old. What distinguishes wishful thinking from careful planning is the absence of any cultivation that would merit being noticed, let alone discovered.

We are sometimes aware of such unresolved aspirations disintegrating us personally. Wayward movements spent satisfying our irresolute intentions are portals into our depletion. They make us feel "small" for giving in to our "petty" side.

We noted earlier that nothing in principle (albeit much in practice) stops us from reckoning the scope of somebody's resolve in terms of the moments of movement comprehended in it. So we feel confident in "sizing people up" and meting out praise or blame accordingly. Consider how the success someone's resolve in comprehending his agency might affect his blameworthiness.

---

[20] William James, *The Varieties of Religious Experience* (New York: Penguin Books, 1981) p. 321.

Suppose that you were called upon to judge two former Nazi death camp prison guards, one a zealot for the cause who integrated himself wholeheartedly into the Party organization, the other who joined the Party to protect his family from persecution. The zealot signed up for camp duty enthusiastically, volunteered to advise the local Party youth club, and sold Nazi magazines door to door. Moreover, he thoroughly enjoyed his ties to the tight community of co-believers with whom he shared a sense of actively inaugurating a thousand year Reich. The other guard hated his job and hated himself for doing it, he did favors for inmates when he could get away with it, his party membership was perfunctory, and he didn't take its historical mythology seriously, and thoughts of his camp duties often kept him sleepless at night.

Each of them, we would agree, bore personal responsibility for what he did inasmuch as his work was part of the way he resolved his life. Just for the sake of argument, let's assume that both guards caused the same amount of personal damage to those they dealt with. (Admittedly, this is a bit of a stretch, but it's at least conceivable that the gung-ho guard was a terrible advisor at the youth club, that he mistakenly turned in his neighbors to the wrong authorities, and that his Doberman ate the list of subscriptions.)

Would we blame them in equal measure? Our sense is that we would not, that we would blame the gung-ho guard more than the anguished one. Whereas he entered wholeheartedly into what he did, the latter, we might say, "wasn't an *entirely* bad person." He had a countervailing set of intentions that were irreconcilable with what he did on the job. Because they proved so irrepressible, we must count them part of his intentional life. Those good impulses were mostly frustrated by what he thought he had to do under the circumstances to provide for his family. Ironically, the fact that those impulses lurked outside of his resolve both diminished him as a person and diminished his blameworthiness. As Hannah Arendt put it, "a 'good conscience' is enjoyed as a rule only by really bad people, criminals and such, while only 'good people' are capable of having a bad conscience."[21] The anguished guard may not have been one of the "good people," but he was one of the less bad ones.

A is irresolute in C: A is irresponsible for C

Our examples up to now have concerned people who "meant to" do what they did, "meant to" in the robust sense of "were resolved to" defraud their customers, spread vicious rumors, or hack the voting machines, for example. But we also blame people who didn't mean to do what they did. On the face

---

[21] Arendt, Hannah, *The Life of the Mind* (San Diego, New York, London: Harcourt, 1978), p. 5

of it, this sounds paradoxical in terms of our account, for since they were not resolved or "determined" to do what we blame them for we cannot hold them responsible. Character logic does not permit us to blame someone for saying something thoughtlessly, getting into an accident while driving home drunk, or forgetting to do what they promised. If behaving gluttonously, intemperately, or negligently—eating unhealthy foods, giving in to road rage, or neglecting to silence one's device at the chamber concert—are blameworthy ways of behaving even though they lie outside the scope of a person's present resolve, it is incumbent on us to provide a character logical explanation of this apparently counter-intuitive entailment.

This is an old philosophical chestnut: how can it make sense to hold someone responsible for acting irresponsibly? To crack it, we must leverage a formal fissure between the two claims: "A did C (responsibly)" and "A did C (irresponsibly)." We can do that by distinguishing the sets of truth conditions for the two types of character claims. We have already seen that in simple personal responsibility claims (like, Bonnie drove the getaway car, Oliver lied to Congress, Martha traded on insider information) three things have to be true for the claim to be true. It must identify A correctly, it must characterize C correctly, and A must be implicated in C, a relation we found established in their mutual implication. That mutual implication, we said, stems from both A and C being implicit in A's active awareness in the moment of C. A is not personally responsible for C unless all three conditions are met.

Charges of irresponsibility are more complex. While they share the form "A did C," they embed an adverbial modifier, one that implicitly or explicitly indicates how A was resolved at the time of C. I don't just berate myself for having written my pin # on my debit card; I berate myself for *foolishly* having done so. It's not just that the Secretary of Defense sent troops to war without crucial equipment; it's that he *recklessly* did so.

To make sense of these embedded adverbial riders attached to all charges of irresponsibility we have to distinguish two actions, the one that occasioned the charge and an earlier one, that being the projection of resolve wherein A set himself on the personal course he was advancing at the time of C. The two actions are formally distinct in that the one executed earlier was resolved, the one later, not. The irresponsible reveler had not resolved to get into an accident, a promise-forgetting friend was not resolved to forget, and the Secretary of Defense hadn't resolved to send the troops off poorly equipped. But, presumably, each was resolved as a person at the time. The distinctive feature of the resolve informing his active awareness at the time was the *deficiency* manifest in its failure to stop him from doing what he did when it would have been narratively advantageous to have forgone it. It is this earlier moment of action characterized as A's deficient projection of resolve that we blame.

Since C was not an element in that resolve and therefore cannot implicate A, we call both agent and action "irresponsible" with reference to C.

Under this analysis the paradox of being responsible for acting irresponsibly loses its sting. Far from *canceling* blame, by calling A "irresponsible" we *deflect* it to an earlier moment of resolve, one that was governing (deficiently) at the time of C and one that therefore identified A. What is blameworthy about an irresponsible agent's projection of his future action is that it was unnecessarily deficient in some way that allowed for C. If A was reckless and caused an accident, A was deficient in reckoning before the accident; if A was careless, A failed to take care before he did what he did. Whatever deficiency his negligence indicated, he failed to project his course so as to avoid the harm he caused when all the while it was within his good faith narrative possibilities to have done so.

This way of unpacking the logic of irresponsibility reminds us of Aristotle's discussion of negligence. He (like us) addressed the paradox by distinguishing two actions, one before the other, and pointed blame at the earlier of them. But critics point to an awkward problem posed by his way of identifying the earlier blameworthy act. In his view, only *voluntary* acts count as blameworthy and that view led him to assume that the agent must have *decided*, even if only by default,[22] to take on that risk at some earlier time. Critics have pointed to a problem created by characterizing the earlier, culpable act as voluntary. The negative words we use to specify someone's negligence ("reckless," "careless," "thoughtless") explicitly deny an awareness of the acts occasioning the charge. Presumably, one could not voluntarily do what one was not aware of doing. One critic points out that Aristotle's account could accommodate such cases "only if he accepted the daffy slogan 'Not to decide is to decide.'"[23]

It clarifies matters, we think, to substitute "resolute" for "voluntary" in Aristotle's account and identify the blameworthy act as that of projecting deficient resolve. The act that occasioned the charge was presumably done under the reign of a character of personal resolve that was deficient, deficient in that it could have better determined the moment of his risky action, but it did not. His resolve was deficient relative to the greater moment he could have actualized had he deliberated effectively in good faith. "I should have thought twice *before* calling you at midnight when I know you're usually asleep by 11." When I felt the impulse to call you, I should have "thought twice," that is, considered my impulse in the context of your interests, which are accommo-

---

[22] Aristotle, *Nicomachean Ethics* III, 5, 1115.
[23] Sverdlik, Steven (1993) "Pure Negligence" *American Philosophical Quarterly* 30 (2), p.141.

dated in my resolve. Consideration was my imperative because my friendship with you commits me to act in accord with your life.

So, when we blame someone for having acted negligently, we are assuming something about his narrative capacity, namely, that it allowed for another way forward, more momentous and without taking the risk he took. Had he been more present in his resolve at the time, he would have avoided doing C.

Because a reckless person is only reckless against his normal capacity for reckoning, and a thoughtless person against his considerate nature, deficiency of resolve also has its measure. We appraise it as relative to how we imagine the irresponsible person might have advanced his story in good faith in a way that would have avoided the risk of C. There was a volume of his active moment that went un-actualized because of the risk he took. In principle, that volume represents his personal deficiency. A person is responsible for that momentary gap in his active awareness when he acted irresponsibly, and, since it is the *gap* we blame him for, its negative moment determines how much blame we heap upon his head. That gap widens as the risk rises, so while we cannot consider the damage done by irresponsible behavior as a direct factor in determining his blameworthiness (since it was not what he intended), the damage done is reflected indirectly by the weightier claim his risky behavior should have had on his deliberative attention. The great negative moment his intention risked in cases of "gross" negligence should have registered all the more against the way he projected resolve and stopped him short. That makes it all the more blameworthy.

A is no longer narratively coherent with C: A is forgiven for C

Our account of personal responsibility finds its basis in the character connection between an action characterized in the charge and the person charged. When that connection no longer holds, blame becomes irrational. That is because the person we address is no longer implicated in the action charged, his life now being narratively discontinuous with his earlier agency. Our respect for him as the person he is requires us to stop holding his offense against him.

This entailment of our account is bound to invite some objections, both on moral and legal grounds. People do not commonly recognize a moral duty to forgive those who have offended them, nor do they think that anybody has a moral right to be forgiven by those they hurt. And the denial of a legal right to forgiveness is even more emphatic. Reformed convicts may be granted parole before their sentences are up, but when that happens it is regarded as an act of clemency, not an act whereby someone is granted his right.

The question we would press is this: does the denial that forgiveness is a right have a basis in intuition or is this one of those cases of forensic reasoning being distorted by a faulty understanding of personal identity? After all, even though philosophical skepticism has undermined any consensus about personal identity, there is an entrenched conceptual habit of treating a person as an entity rather than a character. That habit makes it reasonable to divorce someone's identity from how he leads his life and to insist that he is and always will be the person who committed the offense. Because he continues to be that offender, it would be irrational to stop holding him responsible for his offense.

But it is category logic, reinforced as it frequently is by an essentialist way of thinking still holding sway over our judgments in this matter. Charles Griswold's work on forgiveness reflects this essentialist commitment. He appreciates that changes can take place in a person's character, changes that might well give us moral grounds for "re-framing" the way we see him, "seeing the offender in a new light." But Griswold insists that the reframing

> does not come to the view that the wrong-doer is not to be considered as being the wrong-doer, to "washing away" the fact of her having done wrong (that would be more like amnesia, or excusing, or condonation (of the sort that claims no wrong was really done)). So it must involve something like distinguishing that "part" of the self responsible for the injury from the "whole" person.[24]

What the wrong-doer did in the past, according to Griswold, is a "part" of him just as what he is doing now is a "part" of him. Thus the character of his present action is only what is presently true of him; it does not of itself identify him. Since the taint on his identity left by his wrongdoing is indelible, on this account, only an amnesiac, excuser, or condoner could stop resenting him. He is and always will be the offender, character changes notwithstanding.

This view of the persons we forgive is not only widely assumed today; it has been for centuries. Bishop Butler set the tone in the 18th century with his seminal work on the topic, which taught that when we forgive someone, even though we forswear taking revenge, we reasonably hold onto our anger and resentment. So entrenched is that understanding that Martha Nussbaum can argue that forgiveness is itself an impediment to opening up a healthy future

---

[24] Charles Griswold, *Forgiveness: A Philosophical Exploration*. (Cambridge: Cambridge University Press, 2007), p. 57.

since it is likely to give the forgiver the means to manipulate the person forgiven by holding his past over him.[25]

But for all its pervasiveness and persistence, the prevailing view cannot accommodate the full interactive meaning of some occasions of forgiveness. For one thing, on such occasions the forgiver and the forgiven are richly present with one another. More than that, they aim to be fully present with one another. There is more going on than an act of foreswearing revenge and an intention to keep one's resentment in check.

To forgive is the opposite of holding back; it is a letting go. What gets let go is precisely the past. Interactions are healthier without offenses hanging between them unalterably. People have needed and people have received forgiveness in which the presence of the person forgiven is no longer the presence of the offender. Hannah Arendt, for one, saw what was at stake:

> Unless we can be released from the consequences of what we have done our capacity to act would, as it were, be confined to one single deed from which we could never recover; we would remain the victims of its consequences forever, not unlike the sorcerer's apprentice who lacked the magic formula to break the spell.[26]

If we recognize the character of a person's presence as his being, we can reasonably hope that both the forgiven and forgiving person will be able to interact without the offense as a sore spot that never quite heals.

On the moral level there is ample testimony to the transformative power of forgiveness in relationships when the forgiver truly lets go of the past and stops holding it against the offender. On the legal level the examples are harder to come by. There are anecdotal reports of reconciliation being effected in countries like South Africa that have undergone political upheavals, but these usually take place apart from the normal judicial institutions. It is difficult to institutionalize forgiveness for reasons that go well beyond conceptual confusion. Even when we are free from the hold of essentialist accounts of identity, there remain towering practical impediments to finding the kind of evidence that could justify legal forgiveness. After all, the only cognitive basis we can have for forgiving someone is a personal knowledge of the continuities and discontinuities in an offender's resolve over time.

---

[25] Martha C. Nussbaum, *Anger and Forgiveness: Resentment, Generosity, Justice* (New York: Oxford University Press, 2016), p. 124

[26] Hannah Arendt, *The Human Condition*. (Chicago: The University of Chicago Press, 1958), p. 237.

Judges and parole boards have to base their judgments on secondary sources—the testimony of psychiatrists, wardens, etc.— and even that testimony must depend for the most part on overt behavior. But it is important to distinguish these practical difficulties in determining when forgiveness makes sense from conceptual ones. When a convict is presently resolved in a way that is narratively discontinuous with his criminal self, that is an objective truth about him, and it not only legitimizes forgiveness but makes it his right. So when judges have it on good, albeit indirect, authority that a convict has resolved his life anew so that he can forswear exploiting others in good faith, they would be justified in wiping the legal slate clean. Anything less for a convict who actually turned his life around would be a travesty of justice.

A has no personal story: A is not personally responsible

When somebody has no story he cannot be implicated personally in what he does, which means that we cannot reasonably blame him personally. We cannot, for instance, hold children personally responsible for their actions. It might make sense to put protective constraints on them and to correct their behavior, but it never makes sense to punish them. For the same reason, we do not punish people who suffer cognitive deficiencies such that they cannot project, and therefore cannot advance, a personal story. Neuroscience has developed to the point that it may be able to identify physical correlates of personal maturity, but for now these remain inexact. Even if neuroscientists succeed at identifying the neurological conditions for "impulse control," it is useful to keep in mind that the only truly effective impulse control is grounded in personal resolve. It is someone's distinctive imaginative feat in determining his resolve that provides the sufficient condition for his personal responsibility.

To judge that somebody should be tried as a "responsible adult," we would need evidence of the integrative imagination we found earlier marking one's maturity out of adolescence. Yet such evidence can only be established person to person, and that makes it difficult for institutions to accredit. So, to distinguish the juvenile justice system from the criminal justice system, we fall back on chronological age as our criterion. Obviously, the emergence of someone's active awareness as an integral being does not predictably happen on his 18th birthday, so our chronological standard is at best an expedient approximation. The effect of adopting it though is to detach legal concern from the imaginative feat the age criterion is meant to approximate. This in turn makes our reasoning about the age of responsibility vulnerable to the lure of an alternative measurable determinant, the heinousness of the crime. This measure, however, cannot conceivably be thought to approximate the age of responsibility. The ability to form resolve is in no way indicated by the ability to intend a very damaging crime. It is important to call out the vengeful impulse behind the application of this standard if we are even to approximate delivering justice fairly.

We have been reflecting on various issues concerning personal responsibility. What we have found suggests that the intuitive judgments we make do seem to reflect recognition of the mutual character entailment of action and actor. This connection makes personal responsibility coextensive with someone's movement in the character of his resolve. Simply put, all and only what one does resolutely determines the range of one's personal responsibility.

Chapter 5

Personal Integrity

We have been looking at the intuitions that inform moral and legal reasoning, the patterns of inference that reflect our identification of persons by the sense we have of their character of resolve. To the extent we can make a person's character explicit, we tell his personal story, the one that establishes its privileged domain over his agency for as long as it actualizes him most momentously. Because a person's identity is the byproduct of that imaginative feat, its character distinctively names who he is.

We offer this formal description of personal identity to counter an assumption—widely held by people who think systematically about human behavior—that narrative accounts cannot do what we need accounts of personal identity to do, namely, to pick out individual *beings*. According to that assumption, whatever rhetorical coherence a narrative account may confer upon somebody's life, it has no ontological purchase. We are challenging that assumption by pointing out that we denominate our ontological purchases in two currencies, the *real* and the *actual*, the *real* for its measurable purchase on what happens in the world governed by causal relations, the *actual* for its measurable purchase on the being of intentional movement. The former measures with clocks and measuring rods, the latter by assessing the relative volume of intention-satisfying movement promised by the various courses a person might take. The payoff for careful deliberation over alternatives is the achievement of the most momentous intentional satisfaction, which is the only measure of success appropriate to a multi-intentioned agent. Personal success is therefore quantifiable in principle according to the moments of movement determined in character by one's present resolve.

Following the character logical understanding of resolute movement, we came to see that a person's being is not limited to the movement of his body. Instead, it permeates the being of those with whom he interacts. Moreover, the character of what he does (individually or interactively) has historical importance if it extends the movement he makes in accord with his own resolve into action he makes possible in others' lives in the future. That makes all three registers of actual being factors in the measure of his being as a person. Finally, in applying this paradigm, we found what we think is an elegant congruence of rights and responsibilities with the sphere of movement that actualizes the present character of a person's resolve.

Yet it would be premature to unfurl the "Mission Accomplished" banner just yet. The coherence of this account can only jell if we can solve a problem we have deferred several times. At junctures along the way, you will recall, we had to admit that certain inferences we intuitively make are not entirely justified by the axioms of character logic recognized so far. One way the problem posed itself was with reference to our intuitive sense that it is right to put convicts in prison for their crimes. Our account requires that persons (by virtue of what it means to be a person) have the right to opt out of any interactive arrangement that threatens to diminish them. Since putting people behind bars is designed to diminish their lives in comparison to what they would have enjoyed were they still "at large," a person convicted of a crime would almost certainly claim his personal right to absolve from the interactive association that imposed his sentence. This suggests that our intuitive sense of justice in imprisoning law-breakers involves denying them their personal rights.

The anomaly this sort of case generates, namely, of both respecting a convicted person's right to absolve and claiming the right to sentence him against his will, was one of those loose ends we were not prepared to tie up. The other one—which is related to the first—is that every person-respecting society assumes it should give precedence to one person's absolute right over another's positive one. Our account has it that every person has the right, by virtue of his multi-intended agency, to actualize himself in the most momentous way he can. That leaves open the possibility that a person's most momentous life might involve exploiting others. On what grounds can we reject his right to exploit others if that is what, from his perspective, it takes to maximize his moment?

We have been able to pose a provisional answer to these questions by observing that *if* persons can only actualize themselves best in healthy interactive lives, no one can legitimately claim the right to exploit others. But of course that is a big *if*. In this chapter, we are going to consider whether that belief—which we will call the axiom of moral integrity—can be put on a rational footing. Though it might not seem immediately apparent, a great deal rides on this issue. We are going to see in chapter 6 that resolving that paradox does more than tie up a loose end or two philosophically. Some of the most important protocols of a person-respecting, person-fostering society would be in danger of losing their footing if we cannot affirm belief in the possibility of personal integrity.

But examining its basis will involve more than the deductive exercise we have used to explore personal rights and responsibilities. In those discussions we found that the intuitive inferences we draw are reflective of our respect for persons as present characters of resolve. Here, however, we are exploring an axiom that cannot be inferred from our analysis of persons as resolute beings, so we are going to have to take a more indirect approach. It turns out that when humanity began to grasp personal identity in terms of a character of resolve, it did so in a way that connected (character logically) personal identity with the possibility of living in moral integrity. Indeed, when humans began to characterize individuals as bearers of personal stories, they found the possibility of living in moral integrity implicit in that bearing.

More than antiquarian interest justifies our looking closely at the formal construction of these early chapters in the history of personhood. In examining these early chapters, we believe we can discern the form of the evidence those people depended on when they affirmed belief in moral integrity.

It may help at this point to distinguish our approach to the question of moral integrity from the standard one. Philosophers who have explored the relations between personal integrity and morality have reached a consensus that we have no basis for recognizing integrity as intrinsically moral. But what that consensus stems from is an assumption that someone's integrity represents an unwavering adherence to some principle, ideal, or commitment. Viewing integrity as a category of action (like, telling the truth, being loyal to friends, or sticking to non-violence) makes it reasonable to count someone as a person of integrity "even if we were to find his ideal morally abhorrent"[27] or if he were "someone who ruthlessly and without regard for the well-being of others pursues his own aim, even if in doing so he behaves in ways we regard as morally wrong."[28] Integrity in this view could be built around either moral or immoral categories of action. That being the case, the notion that a person of integrity is intrinsically moral must be discounted as a habit of speech with no reasonable grounding.

Against the prevailing assumption that a life of integrity is a principled life, our account analyzes a life of integrity as a life in which the agent is completely resolved. A person of integrity is present whenever someone's personal story integrates her agency comprehensively. Of course, this code shift in how we think of "integrity" does not by itself connect it with morality. We can only make that connection if we depend on the axiom we are interrogating here. Whether integrity has moral as well as personal value depends on whether it is reasonable to believe that *personal wholeness is possible, but only in interpersonally healthy relationships.*

---

[27] McFall, Lynne (1987) "Integrity," p. 14 *Ethics* 98.
[28] Taylor, Gabriele (1981) "Integrity," *Proceedings of the Aristotelian Society Supplement* 55, p. 159.

While this shift does not make integrity moral, it permits, as we said, reasoning about moral integrity in terms of the formal claim it makes about personal resolve. It makes it possible to ask what evidence we would need to affirm the moral integrity of someone's life. It is the character logical determination of what counts as evidence for moral integrity that we hope to discover during the brief excursion into ancient history on which we are about to embark.

How humans came to identify themselves as individual characters of resolve

Identity as an individual character of resolve announced itself in the stories told by Abrahamic monotheists. It was in that lore that persons emerged with a capacity for moral integrity intrinsic to their formal identity. The way the Abrahamic stories and the habits of thought they fostered made sense of personal integrity grew out of something distinctive in their narrative logic. They were not framed as personal stories in the way we have been using that expression. They did not focus on a protagonist like Gilgamesh or Oedipus. Rather they were stories of a relationship of persons, one that either flourished in a healthy partnership (a "covenant") or was broken by one party who absolved and thereby destroyed the partnership, at least temporarily. Moreover, one party to the relationship bore a formally distinct character of resolve: it was *wholly* integrated, a status that justified calling its character "holy."

In the narrative logic governing these early monotheistic tales, the relationship between the human person and the holy person was such that when the partnership flourished the human party was holy too. In times of absolution the relationship fell into discord. But in times of obedience the tellers of those tales understood themselves to be whole/holy in their acts of actualizing God's resolve for their history.

To highlight the special function of the Abrahamic stories—that function being to make their tellers whole—we will distinguish any stories that have this special quality as "Stories," the upper-case 'S' setting them apart from other personal stories. Such Stories purport to completely integrate those who project their lives in the advancement of them. Success in achieving personal wholeness is thus both the testimony of the Storytellers and the action of the Story.

To understand this person-integrating function of Stories and the departure in human thinking they represented, it helps to compare them with other ancient storytelling traditions that represented human agency. Ironically, the word "person" stems from one of those non-Abrahamic storytelling traditions, one founded in the theatrical world of ancient Greece and Rome. In that setting the word may have designated the *sound* coming *through* the mouth of an actor's mask, the *per-sonic* disclosure of a character of dramatic action.

Yet, the defining feature of these classical *dramatis personae* is that they could not be identified as *individual* characters of action. Their *protagony* was a struggle for character individuality, but always in vain because the gods put them under irreconcilable demands and made it impossible to partner with one god without offending another. Should Agamemnon sacrifice his baby daughter to Artemis for winds to speed his journey to Troy? Or should he spare his daughter, insulting Apollo and jeopardizing his fleet? Whatever impossible combination of Olympic hissy fits and/or Dionysian compulsions imposes its obligations on a protagonist, it fates him to fail in his bid to resolve his intentional life. His agony, etched on his mask and orchestrated in the contentions swirling around him, mimics his disintegration; because he dared step forth from the chorus and presumed to speak as an individual, he has to be pulled apart ritually and devoured by the irresolvable narratives he was enlisted to advance.

That these protagonists are fated to fail to emerge as resolved characters is what these plays were about; the imaginative feats they represented were chanted and danced around a Dionysian altar celebrating precisely that impossibility. The cosmic irony experienced by those who told and heard these stories was founded in an awareness of themselves as somatically singular multi-intentioned agents who were fated to press toward resolution but never to achieve it. They could see, just as we can see, that a single character of resolve is every human's natural ideal, even for those whose polytheism makes the quest futile. (Some Asian religions, in stark contrast with Storytellers, promise to do away with intentional strife by advising that all intentions be expunged.) While polytheism was undermining the emergence of individual identity as a character of resolve in Europe, Hebraic monotheism was facilitating it in West Asia. By recognizing only one character of whole/holy being, the Stories removed the barrier posed by divine contentions and opened up the possibility of character individuality.

We should note, however, that at the start of their Storytelling tradition the emergence of individuality did not take place in individual human bodies. The first person was not Adam; it was Israel, a corporate individual identifying a confederation of nomadic tribes. God was whole/holy in the sense of being of one mind, steadfast in upholding obligations under the covenant. By the transitivity of resolve in partnership, that same whole/holiness was bestowed upon Israel, God's personal partner, but only in her moments of acting comportably with God's will (read: resolve). And so, as the Story goes, whenever Israel was coordinated in and with the Character of God's action, the confederated tribes acted as one, the poor and the rich cared for one another, cultic life was pure, dynasties continuous, nature benevolent, and battles victorious. But whenever she absolved from projecting God's Story, she disintegrated. "Going after false gods" meant stumbling in battle, falling into political strife. It meant being invaded, conquered, even reduced to a remnant. Because Yahweh forgave and restored, the Story alternated between periods of apostasy and dissolution and periods of obedience and corporate health, a tick-tock of sacred history: absolution and reconciliation, dismembering and remembering.

In later iterations of this Story, somatically individuated beings like us emerged as personally individual and came to represent the paradigm for personhood we use today. One might even venture to say that the action of the Story required somatically individual persons to emerge. Because Israel's very being was in the covenant, in times of apostasy and dissolution her being came into question. Storytellers took to reasoning that during those dark times Israel's status as God's partner could be maintained in the lives of a few faithful members of Israel, the "prophets" foremost. These somatic individuals maintained the covenant by absolving from and setting themselves against the disintegrating corporate person. In their judgments and jeremiads they proclaimed that Israel had absolved from God's will and had thus lost her basis for integrity and thereby brought upon herself the dissolution she was about to suffer. By continuing to be covenant partners as human individuals, these prophets represented non-corporate characters of holy resolve, the first somatically individuated holy persons.

Israel's eventual messianic expectation also came to be projected by this narrative logic. In times of seemingly irreversible corporate dissolution (like those under Alexander's generals and Rome's governors), wholeness in the person of an individual human suggested itself as the only promising narrative possibility for continuing the Story's advancement. Such times invited and even compelled Storytellers to look for deliverance from dissolution in the person of somebody endowed not only with personal grace but with the power of healing—which is to say, the power of spreading wholeness to others.[29] That accomplishment alone could re-establish corporate personal wholeness in a Kingdom of God. Thus the central proclamation by the Christian movement fixes that very accomplishment in history and proclaims a first-century rabbi as the very Character of God in person among us.

The practice of identifying somatic individuals as whole persons gained more traction in the Christian era, but now in the form of a three-way partnership among God, the incorporated church, and its members. All three

---

[29] "Holy," "whole," and "heal" all seem to derive from the same Old English word, *hailo*.

parties told the Story (or, in the case of God, "inspired" it) and all of them acted to advance it. Because the new Movement celebrated wholeness both in the individual and in their ecclesiastical coordination, when someone was "full of grace" she bore integrity both among her (somatically indexed) intentions and inter-personally as a member of the living "body of Christ."

One finds rich variety in the New Testament depictions of this emerging individual wholeness. The gospels picture it as the exorcism of divisive demons, as holy occasions of healing, and as the raising and rising from the dead. It was not problematic for them (as it is for us) to signify personal wholeness in terms of physical wholeness since Biblical writers had not yet learned to distinguish truths about natural events from truths about actions. In the Book of Acts, the creation of individual wholeness is explicitly narrated as finding actualization in sync with corporate wholeness: those gathered at Pentecost were collectively touched by the Spirit of *Wholeness,* the *Holy* Spirit, and in that very Moment released into a holy idiocy of languages. Paul recognized this tandem identity of inner grace and perfect fellowship as a "new creation," the active occasion of an individual member being incorporated into the risen body of Christ. And so the Eucharist came to celebrate individuals acquiring identity in and as the presence of Christ's body arisen, their new corporate being. At that moment, they enjoyed both inner peace and perfect communion.[30]

Prospects for Integrity in a post-Storytelling Era

This brief foray into the history of individuality as a character of resolve was meant to highlight how the original character logic of "person" equated "integrity" and "morality." Our purpose in highlighting certain features of the paradigm of personal identity was to raise the question of evidence for belief in moral integrity in a more useful way. We saw that the paradigm we have been using up to now is not sufficient for Storytelling since it allows for the personal resolve used to identify persons in forensic contexts to be diminished by zones of agency operating outside of the scope of personal resolve.

---

[30] In much of traditional Islam (as in Ancient Judaism) personal integrity seems more derived from communal roles than from idiosyncratic projection. If that is true, one can see why western political ideologies sound counter-intuitive to traditional Muslims. To foster democracy across sectarian lines requires individuals to assert rights against the communal order, and that requires exercising a more freely fictive imagination than the strict protocols of a tightly coordinated communal order can allow.

This "sin" of partiality in the identity of personal agency is so universal that many Storytellers call it "original." It represents someone's partial dissolution, not only as a multi-intentioned agent but as a party to unhealthy relationships. To represent the character logic of a Story we have to complement the paradigm of partially resolved personhood with one representing an entirely resolved intentional life, someone who is *whole* in the sense that her story entirely comprehends her active life. Such a story would be of someone who enjoys interactive health, and whose resolve is narratively given to the accomplishment of wholesomeness in history. Because Storytellers identify themselves with both of these paradigms, they are aware of themselves as partial ("fallen," "sinful") persons and as persons who have available to them a life of wholeness. With Augustine they confess to being *peccator* as well as *justus*, each negotiating (if you will permit us the full play of our idiosyncratic use of gendered pronouns) an interface between her momentarily actualized wholeness and his oft-times actual partiality.

If we are right in tracing belief in personal integrity to the sense of identity fostered by monotheism, we seem to have put belief in moral integrity in jeopardy. The monotheistic traditions have ebbed as a tide of history and, as we have seen, so has the coherence of the belief itself. This sea change will suggest to some that we should perhaps accept that "moral integrity" is an implausible if not meaningless conceit in our post-Storytelling era. But this forfeiture, as we will see, has its costs. Giving up the belief that a life of moral integrity is everyone's possibility cannot but degrade our person-respecting society.

One might try to salvage a rational belief in moral integrity by trying to find some other way to make sense of it and some other basis for believing in it. But precisely this strategy is the one that has led to skepticism about moral integrity since the only alternative to a narrative account of it seems to be a category account and the consensus seems to be that integrity so understood cannot be tied to morality.

Instead of giving up on moral integrity, we hope to reaffirm the claims about the form personal resolve can take when they are embodied in the old Stories without affirming what people today find unbelievable about those Stories. Our strategy will be to distinguish the actual claims they make from the factual ones; it's the latter that are unbelievable to modern ears. Evidence for the formal claims, it turns out, is different from the factual evidence widely thought to confirm or disconfirm the Stories. By showing why factual evidence can neither confirm nor disconfirm the truth of a putative Story, we can discern them in a way that shows us what kind of evidence they were depending upon when they claimed to be telling narrative truth.

The distinction between factual and formal conditions for the truth of a character claim in a personal story needs some explaining and defending. If we are able to draw it clearly, we will see that the usual reasons people give for rejecting the purported truth of Stories are based on a set of misconceptions about the truth of storytelling in general, about the truth of personal storytelling in particular, and even more particularly about the truth of Storytelling.

The most common argument against truth in Storytelling

To tell a Story, you will recall, is to narrate a life of perfect integrity both in the teller's being as a multi-intentioned agent and in her being as an interactor with other persons. The truth of a Story is a function of whether it actually integrates the teller's intentional life and maintains her interactive health. The truth of a Story, therefore, makes it axiomatic that the most fully actualized life is one that pursues healthy personal relationships.

None of these matters to those whose only concern is with factual truth. For them, once a Story has been exposed as factually false it counts as fiction. Once it has been shown that the Story's narration of what happened simply could not have happened, the notion of truth in Storytelling becomes, for that sort of skeptic, a non-starter. They would hold that our category reasoning—anthropological, archeological, zoological, psychological, and the like—about how things happen in the world shows that what the "Stories" say happened could not have happened. Regardless of whether Storytellers think they are telling the truth, this line of reasoning continues, they must be mistaken.

This section of the chapter is addressed to people inclined to such skepticism. We are going to argue that the reasoning that persuades people that alleged Stories cannot be true misconstrues how the truth of personal stories relates to factual truth. It confuses claims about the actual with claims about the factual.

When we hear news stories, police arrest reports, trial testimonies, and excuses for why someone was late to work, we rightly insist that such stories are believable only if they stick to the facts. But if one is thinking about personal stories, a little reflection reveals that departures from strict factuality are more the norm than the exception. This, we are going to see, is because there is an unavoidable tension between person-disclosing narratives and strictly realistic ones. By reminding ourselves of how we become aware of this tension and how we relieve it, we position ourselves to understand why the peculiar challenge of Storytelling requires stretching the facts beyond even the pretense of factuality.

Since distorting facts in the interest of personal disclosure is in some respects an extension of the kinds of distortions we countenance in simple impersonal characterizations, we might look first at how readily we resort to factual exaggerations in characterizing someone's actions. Think for example of those celebrity "roasts" where the glitterati regale one of their own by telling outlandish tales about him. Everybody knows that the tall tales are not meant to deceive anyone but only to poke fun at the honoree. Why does the raconteur take liberties with the factual truth? The simple answer is that he knows the stories wouldn't be as funny if he didn't. But he also knows that the stories wouldn't be funny if they didn't have a ring of truth to them. By using exaggeration to sharpen the characterization of an (allegedly) true claim about the roasted celebrity's public persona the roaster skewers him all the better. E. H. Gombrich pointed out a comparable dynamic in political cartooning. A caricature succeeds, he said, "because its lack of elaboration guarantees the absence of contradictory clues."[31] Recall, if you can, how *Washington Post* editorial cartoonist Herblock evoked the truth of Richard Nixon's character through selective distortion.

To be sure, roasted celebrities are only public personae, and they are unlikely to be revealed in much of their personal richness on those occasions. So, to get at how factual distortion can enhance the disclosure of *personal* being, let us propose a little thought experiment. Since persons are typically disclosed by what they do over time, let us imagine a library of historical accounts of notable people. They all purport to be truth-telling accounts rendered in the past tense. Now let us divide our library into two sections. On one side we will put accounts of what people did in a manner meant to disclose them as persons: we will call these accounts biographies. On the other side we will put accounts with a different authorial intent. Their goal is to support certain hypotheses about what really happened, about how events unfolded in history. We will call these critical histories. Both biographies and critical histories include narratives of what people did. They both contain past tense character claims. But they use character claims differently. When a critical history narrates what someone did, it filters out the personal meaning his action had for him. When biography narrates what someone did, it sometimes takes liberties with the facts surrounding what he did in the interest of disclosing the personal truth of that action.

We can illustrate the impersonalization of critical history with a celebrated chapter in Thucydides' history of the Peloponnesian War, the chapter in which he recounts the Athenian leader Pericles' funeral oration. Thucydides'

---

[31] E. H. Gombrich, *Art and Illusion* (Princeton and Oxford: Princeton University Press Bollingen Series XXXV 5, 2000), p. 336.

narrative purpose was to recount a speech that he believed was a recital of the civic ideals that he, Thucydides, thought Athens had betrayed as the war dragged on. He believed that this betrayal helped to account for Athens' loss. In Thucydides' critical historical project, Pericles' speech draws a causal connection between a polis betraying its ideals and losing its wars. Given that this was the dedicated function of Thucydides' depiction of Pericles' speech, any attempt to disclose the speaker's resolute presence in what he said would have been distracting. Had the historian been an eye-witness to the occasion, he might have picked up on a certain political edge to what Pericles was saying, a barbed allusion to the non-democrats in attendance, perhaps a coded assurance to other constituencies. But to relate any such intentional richness, even in terms of the archon's political resolve (much less in the more comprehensive reaches of personal meaning the occasion had for him), would have been beside the point. For his critical purposes, "what happened" in the speech was a rehearsal of Athenian ideals; its personal richness had to be hidden in the shadows to highlight that factual point.

With biography—that other section of our library—the point of narrating action is to characterize how the subject put his life together. Owing to that distinctive authorial purpose, there is a comparable tendency to sacrifice strict factual accuracy. Because "critical biographers" resist this tendency as a matter of principle, they count, in terms of our distinction, as critical historians. But it has to be admitted that, because they relate the life of their subject without embellishing the facts, they are somewhat impeded in disclosing the richness of their subject's personal character. Critical biographers often have to characterize their subject's actions as though they were discrete moves, leaving the reader to make a much greater imaginative leap if he is to grasp the intentional consonance discrete actions had in the subject's personal life.

The only real limit to a biographer's distortion of reality is that he must not thereby distort the personal character of the action portrayed (as do fictional biographies like Shakespeare's history plays). The biographer's goal is to highlight the intentional complexity and coherence of his subject. Perhaps film biographies illustrate most vividly the challenge strict adherence of facts would pose. They scramble events and stretch facts in the interest of depicting a subject's coherence or incoherence more clearly. They put people together when and where they hadn't really been together, they give them dialogue more succinct than they really spoke, or they collapse some of their most personally important accomplishments into a few emblematic moves. But though they gloss over most of the interruptions and temporary reversals their subject suffered along the way, the cuts, glosses, and chronological distortions are justified *if and only if they disclose the person better*. They must make the narrative *truer* to his personal story, truer to who he is.

There is another, less obvious type of fact-bending people use to enhance the narrative truth of personal disclosure, one that is rarely remarked upon. Particularly in autobiography there is the possibility of conveying the momentousness of personally important actions by magnifying some of the facts surrounding them. A personal experience of one of us (Prust) can be used to illustrate this. It was brought back to me when I read an autobiography by historian, playwright, and gay activist, Martin Duberman. In it he describes a long series of well-meaning but futile psychiatric attempts to make him "straight." At the very end of the book (called *Cures*[32]), he recalls a party that he and his partner attended in the early '70s. The episode is biographically important because it describes a celebration of the real "cure" that all the false ones had impeded along the way. That night he finally felt free to be "out" at a presumptively straight dance party at St. Andrews University (then College) in Laurinburg, NC, where he had been a visiting historian (and where this writer long and happily taught). I can confirm Duberman's report that the party-goers (I among them) burst into applause when he and his partner took to the dance floor and then let out an even bigger Whoop a few minutes later when a male student cut in.

Because Duberman found that moment joyously liberating he adopted it as the emblem of his being "cured" and, in the closing pages, used it to resolve his personal story at that stage of its telling. As I read his account I could almost relive that party; he captured it that well. What made it so memorable for me was that it was a great communal moment for all of us in attendance, as well as an emblematic one for Duberman. While the rest of us could not have known much of its personal significance for him, we were aware of it as a healing moment for us all.

But as I read his account I also noticed some atmospheric exaggeration. The party did not take place in the college dining room but in a smaller main lounge of a residence hall. The hall has three floors, not five. The beer kegs weren't "gigantic," just regular size. Now, by pointing to these exaggerations I do not mean to niggle over Duberman's recollections; quite the contrary, I am suggesting that we read these tiny inflations in the field of action as gestures toward the great moment of what was happening. The hall had five floors and the kegs were gigantic for us all that night. The pumped-up frothy exuberance of the occasion bespoke the volume of intentional living being resolved in our communal space; we fancied then and know now that we were advancing in history a wider culture of acceptance. That is what actually happened that night, and reality simply had to be stretched a bit to express such great moment.

---

[32] Martin Duberman, *Cures: A Gay Man's Odyssey* (NY: Penguin, 1991).

We have been looking at some of the benign ways we find facts creatively altered in the interest of representing resolve so that its character and moment come through more truly. The relevance of these tendencies to our point about Stories and factuality is perhaps already clear. Because the resolve characterized in a Story is whole/holy, the tension between act and fact is exponentially heightened. We saw earlier that the reason children's stories tend to sacrifice factual plausibility is that an enchanted world displays the arcs of important actions better to a young imagination. Something akin to that pragmatic advantage seems to account for the pull of the fantastic in narratives characterizing whole/holy action. Ancient writers perceived what was happening on much the same level of realism as present-day children; they understood the world largely as a field of actions impeded only by other actions. Nature was for them, as it once was for each of us, an arena where the character of somebody's action determines all the important things that happen. That made it natural for them to make the real world malleable in the interest of disclosing perfect integrity, interactive health, and ultimate historical importance. Ironically, one can even say that it was *because* those first Storytellers had not yet developed the conceptual tools to understand nature as a system of causes and effects that their legacies continue to be compelling now. Their heuristic power depends on their factual naiveté. What was natural for them remains necessary for us if there is to be Storied truth: a Storyteller can only narrate a Character of graceful personhood in narratives unimpeded by the complications of causes and effects.

We noted earlier that there is a limit to how much license with the facts a biography can take, that it expires when it fails to improve the disclosure of the personal character and the actual moment of the occasion. The same holds true for Stories, which distinguishes them from what we usually think of as myths. Whereas Stories purport to tell what actually happened at a certain time and place, the actions myths narrate take place outside of historical time. Personal Stories purport to narrate historical occasions when a Character of Wholeness acted in a "fullness" of time, that is, in a saturated moment, one in which people were aware of divine accomplishment taking place in their midst. A Story is thus tied to reality but not accountable to factuality.

Evidence for and against moral integrity

The previous section tried to fend off a popular argument that attempts to debunk Storytelling by exposing its failure to track real occurrences. By way of a counterargument, we suggested that those who debunk Storytelling in this manner fail to distinguish actual from factual truth. Our argument was meant to clear some of the underbrush that obscures evidence that, by the standards of character logic, can indeed confirm a putative Story as true or disconfirm it as false.

Here we reach the pivot of this chapter and, in some ways, the book. Having conceded that moral integrity cannot be immediately inferred from the outline of character logic we have presented so far, we still have it incumbent on us to show how the connection between personal integrity and moral integrity can be established by reason operating with evidence.

If Abrahamic Stories and their offspring were the only source and justification for belief in moral integrity, its prospects would diminish as its historical underpinnings lost their credibility. But this needn't happen. The account that follows is intended to preserve the formal truth of the ancient narrative while discarding the potentially objectionable contents. That way we will be better able to make clear the truths that base belief in moral integrity.

Before presenting this account, let us remind ourselves what is at stake. We are not the first to fear that respect for persons might be ebbing. Of the numerous speculative visions of a post-personal world, Aldous Huxley's *Brave New World* is a particularly poignant warning. While there are those who could accept such a world, B.F. Skinner, the author of *Beyond Freedom and Dignity*, possibly numbering among them, Huxley's dystopian vision is enough to convince most of us that a post-personal future would be undesirable. When we contrast two possible futures, one a world that permits individuals to actualize themselves by exercising personal resolve and the other a world that does not, most of us, we trust, would opt for the former. Even if we acknowledged the various threats to world peace and stability posed by wayward individuals, most of us would resist a social transformation that channeled choice into the hands of a committee of social engineers.

This need not be our destiny. We believe that the lessons learned from the Abrahamic tradition, when mined for their formal significance, generate a rational foundation for belief in moral integrity and therefore a rational foundation for our moral and legal intuitions. Moreover, we believe that the thesis we are about to present can be assessed for its truth value by any moderately sensitive individual. Worth repeating here is that we are not considering the truth-telling or lack thereof of any particular putative Story, ancient or new. Rather, our aim is to determine what kind of evidence it would take to substantiate a Story claim, that is, a claim that someone's personal story achieved the complete integration of her intentional life.

Notwithstanding our claim that the truth of a Story's character claims is not a function of the truth of its factual claims, there is no denying that the factual arguments against Storytelling as truth-telling have largely won the day in the broader intellectual arena. Yet, at the same time, the force of skepticism has been largely unsuccessful in supplanting the natural longing people have to tell a Story. Since only a Story registers ultimate moment in all three registers of personal being, we aspire to tell one just because we are multi-intentioned agents by nature.

This puts those of us who are modern seekers in a bind: though we yearn to tell a Story, we may be too intellectually sophisticated to do so, or too mindful of our hearers' intellectual sophistication. Thus many can only tell or hear it when it is sanitized of any pre-scientific claims. That reduces them to telling a Story in an abstract and highly condensed way. The wide appeal of Martin Luther King Jr's proclamation that "the arc of the moral universe is long, but it bends toward justice" stems from the fact that we hear in that lofty claim the intimation of a Story of communal actions truly bending society toward justice, thus making a momentous advance in the on-going accomplishment of a healthier social order we want to believe is possible. In that truncated form it passes muster by sounding inoffensive to reason. King's proclamation refers implicitly to the Christian Story, albeit without recalling its supernatural setting. The detachment from those moorings allows it to be heard by listeners who can no longer take ancient tales seriously. King's allusion to the narrative arc has the power to awaken hope that there is still a Story to be told even if hard-headed realism prevents many from taking the original narrative seriously.

So much for the wrong-headed reasons for rejecting Storied truth. Now let's consider what the right reasons would be. What kind of evidence could convince a rational person, one way or the other, whether integrity and interactive health were inseparable? What kind of evidence would support a rational belief in the axiom of moral integrity and what kind of evidence would disconfirm that belief?

The most direct way to describe the kind of evidence relevant to belief in moral integrity is to unpack the truth conditions ancient Storytelling requires. To some extent, we have already done this. But to build on what we have found so far, it helps to connect the formal conditions for belief in moral integrity with the formal conditions for belief in ethical monotheism. The latter belief constitutes itself as *theistic, ethical,* and *mono.* As we are analyzing it, these three conditions represent the *formal features we would have to find in the character of personal resolve in order to confirm moral integrity.* To be theistic, in our formal sense of the term, there must be evidence in someone's character of resolve that she is living into a narrative that resolves her life completely: her Story must manifestly make her whole/holy. To be ethical, there must be evidence that she treats others with respect in all of her interactions. And to be mono, the evidence would have to allow for the hope that all Stories are comportable.

Ethical monotheism is equivalent to the conjunction of these three claims about a form someone's character of resolve can take. The evidence we seek—evidence available in principle to any person's active awareness—is evidence that at least one person's story is a Story, that Storytellers never exploit others, and that all Stories can be resolved. If ethical monotheism is to count as a rational belief (in the sense of being confirmed or refuted on the basis of evidence), then we must be able to say what kind of evidence would count for or against each of these three characterizations.

To establish the rationality of theism, we must specify what kind of evidence would establish whether somebody's personal story was (or was not) a Story. That means affirming her as whole (or not), which would mean affirming that the scope of her resolve was (or was not) comprehensive over the whole of her intentional life. Our earlier discussion showed us that someone's presence or absence as a whole person is an objective truth about her or him. Now we are asking whether evidence accessible to people generally could verify this presence. Can any thoughtful person make a *reasonable* judgment about whether somebody he knows well is entirely at one with himself in his active being?

Early on, when we discussed the coordination of actions that constitute resolve, we found it analogous to the coordination of physical movements in the achievement of a graceful athletic or artistic performance. We noted that we make what we take to be reasonable judgments about the latter feats. Take the spectators at an Olympic event: somebody with a close, unobstructed view may feel justified in second-guessing what the judges say about the relative presence or absence of grace in a gymnast's routine, believing that the judges were too stingy or generous in awarding points. We all know coordination when we see it, and we know how to appreciate its levels of achievement.

Given the analogy between awareness of physical grace and awareness of the coordination someone achieves in resolving himself, there are comparable grounds for making reasonable judgments in the latter case. We find in both moves made with a singularity of intentional bearing and coordination achieved in a measure relative to an entire body of intentional movement. That makes us justified in judging that some people have put their lives together relatively well while others appear to be "at odds" with themselves in how they execute their intentions.

There is, to be sure, a difference between our appreciation of intentional coordination in physical and personal bodies of movement. We can assess the former without necessarily reflecting on its components or even characterizing individual moves. Measuring resolve in a person's actions, in contrast, requires that we reflect on his specific undertakings to imaginatively confirm their coordination as elements of his resolve. For that reason, conventional stories only begin to take shape well into their telling, their promise of coherence emerging only gradually. As Michael Polanyi might have put it, attention to physical grace as an integration of physical movement relegates awareness of individual moves to the tacit realm whereas to grasp personal grace we must shift our focus reflexively between the character of individual actions and the character of their resolution.

This pattern of reflexive inference—from the evidence of characterizable movement to the global character of its integration and back again—has its counterpart in the way we reason from individual facts, the data, to the category claims we take them to support, and then back again for continuing confirmation. Both kinds of comprehension involve shifting back and forth between levels of awareness—the evidence and our reading of it—and in both we hold ourselves accountable to each of the two levels. In that sense both kinds of judgment are rational assessments of the success of integral movement.

To judge that there is complete integrity in somebody's agency, we would have to find a core of concord in her intentional movement and the lack of any apparent discord in her agency as a whole. Reportedly, Michael Harrington found such evidence for integrity when he encountered Dorothy Day, the founder of *The Catholic Worker* and a social reformer in New York City during the Depression. She seemed to him

> severe yet serene, and [he] thought she looked like a mystic out of a Dostoevsky novel. She was a presence, he wrote, the sort of person a stranger who had never heard of her would know was significant as soon as she entered a room. He counted himself as "one of hundreds of thousands who were influenced by her life."[33]

Severe in her single-mindedness yet serene in the absence of discord: a dual observation formally parallel to the way in which we judge the success of a graceful physical performance. Note that in both types of case, we find evidence of integration in the lack of wayward movement. Whether on the dance floor, the parallel bars, or the skating rink, disintegration is manifest in moves that *disappoint* when they fail to bear optimally on the *appointed* global feat; intentional moves *disappoint* when they divert somebody from his *appointed* path of resolve. Both constitute moments of disintegration.

---

[33] Dan Wakefield, *New York in the Fifties* (NY: St. Martin's Press, 1992), pp. 77-78.

When we are aware of wayward satisfactions in our lives, they register as ambiguous in value. They satisfy an intention of ours (that is, of the somebody we are) so we are aware that they have some positive value, but they also steal moment from the resolute core of our agency, which makes us aware of their negative value. That is why when we satisfy those intentions it is often with a sense of *misgiving,* that is, an awareness of the action as *giving* us some satisfaction that we intend but *mis-giving* us what we are resolved to do. That depletion in our personal being when we behave irresponsibly is what we experience as "guilt."

We conclude from this that it can be *reasonable* to judge the presence or absence of someone's momentary wholeness. Granted, convictions about integrity are far from foolproof, but then judgments about its presence or absence do not have to be infallible to be reasonable.

The second component of ethical monotheism has it that persons of integrity invariably intend to have healthy interactions with others. Only evidence confirming a fixed constellation of personal wholeness and interactive health could be the basis for affirming moral integrity as everyone's character logical possibility. We would have to find evidence that achieving the highest degree of intentional satisfaction—the natural telos of all multi-intentioned agents—never requires people to exploit others. We have to find evidence, in other words, that persons of integrity are always able either to engage others in a healthy way or to disengage in a righteous way. Ethical monotheism can be judged rational only if we find that the more integrated a person's life is, the healthier his relationships are.

Assessing evidence for interactive health does not pose any new challenge since it calls for the same kind of narrative imagination we use in assessing the integrity of individuals. Manifest concord and lack of discord within a multi-intentioned life takes the same form as manifest concord and lack of discord among people interactively. Anyone with a normally nuanced comprehension of action, then, should be able to confirm or disconfirm the ethical tenet of ethical monotheism. Here too, though, we have to admit that no matter how much evidence we have for interactive health, that evidence is never conclusive. A black swan could always swim into view. Moreover, the black swan would be conclusive. All it would take is one wholesome person with a narrative that can only be advanced in good faith by exploiting other people for the second pillar of ethical monotheism to be toppled and for moral integrity to be brought back into disrepute as a reasonable belief.

The third tenet of ethical monotheism is the narrative capacity of all Storytellers to advance their Stories comfortably. We need evidence that any well-informed Storyteller who exercises sufficient wit and wisdom has it within her to interact comportably with other Storytellers, even those with other Stories. This is a crucial belief for ethical monotheists because the incomportability of any two Stories would imply the truth of polytheism, or the formal equivalent of polytheism.

Here too, we would need evidence that people perceived to be persons of integrity can learn to comport with other persons of integrity. Persons of integrity must be able to project their resolve in good faith without diminishing other persons. Even one counterexample would disconfirm the universal comportability of Storytellers.

Trying to show that all Storytellers can comport might seem like a doomed objective from the start. Apparent counter-examples suggest themselves in droves. Who can even count all the religious wars between tribes of self-proclaimed persons of integrity who are implacably committed to one another's demise? But we would be foolish to take such cases at face value. After all, some of them may turn out to be conflicts between storytellers who only claim to be Storytellers. Others may prove to be conflicts among Storytellers that are unnecessary, that could have been resolved if the parties had only understood each other better and been more imaginative in trying to accommodate one another's narrative needs.

The question is whether there are dependable tests for such false positives. We believe there are. If we were able to filter out all the cases involving false claims to be telling a Story and all the cases involving resolvable conflicts among genuine Storytellers, then the absence of any remaining cases would tend to confirm moral integrity. Then and only then we could reasonably hope that all persons of integrity could be true to one another in good faith.

Here too, it would seem that people can make rational judgments on this matter based on evidence available to any narratively imaginative person. If, in principle, we can identify persons of integrity and tell when their respective bodies of intention are comportable, then, in principle, we ought to be able to discern whether two persons of integrity can reconcile their differences.

This may seem too ethereal to contemplate, so let us bring it down to earth by imagining Bea and Jay, back when they were just casual acquaintances, deciding to set up housekeeping together. For each of them, this was a risky move. Neither knew whether it would work out, that is, whether they would be able to accommodate each other's crucial needs. Certainly one condition for "making a go of it" would be for them to understand each other's "ways," particularly those ways likely to require effort at mutual accommodation. When we consider what it takes to harmonize or comport with another's ways, at least one condition seems obvious. I cannot accommodate your action unless I know what you are doing. If you are playing bridge and I am playing canasta, we are not likely to find our game satisfying.

At the more comprehensive level where partners try to enjoy a healthy *personal* relationship, their shared understanding requires more than understanding their coordinated roles in immediate undertakings. It includes the wider bearing in which each resolves his life as a whole. That added dimension to the meaning they share in their life together is manifest in the deference each pays to the other's personal needs. Because the individual resolve of both Bea and Jay contributes to the meaning of their relational movement, any misunderstanding of the meaning of the other's action would tend to undermine their cooperation and perhaps even preclude their relational success.

This practical requirement for sustaining personal comportability—that the partners grasp each other's character of resolve accurately enough to sustain accountability to it—implies that cases in which one or both parties *mischaracterize* the actions of the other have to count as false positives. They provide no evidence of incomportability among whole persons.

People mischaracterizing others' actions fall into two categories, those doing so in ignorance and those doing so intentionally. Those made out of ignorance leave open the possibility that, were the Storytellers disabused of their misunderstandings, they could come to an understanding and find a way to a healthy relationship.

Intentional mischaracterizations present different problems. The paradigm case is that in which someone lies to take advantage of the person he is interacting with. In doing so, he imposes an unhealthy or exploitative interaction. Generalizing from that paradigm, we are justified in concluding that deliberate mischaracterizers cannot count as Storytellers after all.

So if neither naïve nor willful mischaracterizations count against the comportability component of moral integrity, it follows that a genuinely disconfirming case would require two persons of integrity who had an accurate read on each other's character of resolve but still could not in good faith accommodate each other's narrative requirements by either engaging supportively or disengaging respectfully. Just one such case would be sufficient to falsify the "mono" part of "ethical monotheism". That is, for ethical monotheism to qualify as a reasonable belief, every time a putative Storyteller mischaracterizes another's resolve, it will have to turn out either to mark her misinformation or disintegration.

The first category covers a great many cases: misinformation is indeed behind much of the failure of religious traditions to get along. Though cultural isolation also figures, a good deal of the mischaracterization is fostered by people who profit from its propagation. By disparaging other-Storied tribes, wily leaders are often able to cement solidarity in their societies. These mischaracterizations, unlike the mischaracterizations we find in everyday interactions, can be difficult to correct. When self-proclaimed Storytellers confront one another with a legacy of faulty assumptions about how the other is resolved, distrust makes paths to reconciliation elusive. If we can determine that *ignorant* mischaracterizations are operating to make rapprochement impossible in a given case, it would not count against the "mono" part of ethical monotheism.

As to the other category of partnership-precluding mischaracterizations of others' personal stories, the willful kind, it shows by its context of exploitation that it could not come from an ethically monotheistic Storyteller. If we listen to people who use mischaracterizations to exploit or justify exploiting those with whom they interact, we can sometimes hear them signaling their recognition of a duty to have healthy interactions whenever such are possible. Their false justification for exploiting others reveals itself, as La Rochefoucauld put it, in the hypocrisy that vice pays to virtue. In order to create the impression that an unhealthy interaction cannot be held against them, they have to pretend that a healthy one is impossible because of the character of the other's actions.

Thus did self-righteous slaveholders in 19th century America choose to think that their human "property" had the mentality of children who could understand only the simplest intentions. Their willful mischaracterization precluded interaction between masters and slaves based on mutual personal respect. After the U.S. Civil War and the abolition of slavery, former slaves were legally recognized as rightful citizens. Instead of moving toward conditions of interaction that would have been appropriate for a person-respecting society, new willfully concocted mischaracterizations emerged to justify further exploitation. The doctors in the infamous Tuskegee Study experimented on African-Americans by allowing their syphilis to go unchecked just to see how its course might run. By representing their experimental subjects as sexually promiscuous, ignorant, and prone to syphilis anyway, they tried to convince themselves and others that the suffering of their subjects was nothing beyond what they would have suffered anyway. By characterizing their subjects in this manner, they attempted to show that their interaction was not exploitative.

Alternatively, people can mischaracterize their own actions to excuse what would otherwise be regarded as exploitation. The Nazis reportedly fostered the beliefs, "that the war was no war; …that it was started by destiny and not by Germany; and…that it was a matter of life and death for the Germans, who must annihilate their enemies or be annihilated."[34]

These two categories of false characterizations—the naïve and the willful—often overlap, and one often sees an oscillation between them. The claim that "Saddam is stockpiling weapons of mass destruction" might have been made because the Bush administration was getting bad information. It also might have been made willfully in an effort to justify attacking Iraq. But in all probability, there was an element of both, interpreting the intelligence data to see what they needed to see to justify the attack. Most 19th-century slave owners both could not and would not see the person Huck Finn saw in Jim, and the "could not" and the "would not" fed into an equilibrium racists find unable/unwilling to disturb even today.

In any case, putative Storytellers' mischaracterizations—whether ignorant, vicious or both—prove nothing against belief in moral integrity. But do all apparent conflicts between Storytellers involve either a willful pseudo-Storyteller or an innocently ignorant actual Storyteller? Our argument is that if it is rational to hold that these are the only two possibilities, it is also rational to believe that the only counterexamples to our thesis are false positives. If that proves the case, we have reason to hope for universal comportability among persons of integrity, which would allow the axiom of moral integrity to qualify as rational.

Your patience with the turn our argument has taken in this chapter may have worn somewhat thin by now. You may think that it is not a particularly crucial matter whether belief in moral integrity can be confirmed or disconfirmed by universally available evidence. Perhaps you are inclined to settle for the "partial" person paradigm we found sufficient for most moral and legal reasoning. Perhaps you take moral integrity for granted, believing that we can depend on conceptual inertia or on some as yet unforeseeable evolutionary advance. Perhaps you are confident we can sustain a person-respecting, person-fostering society without drawing water from ancient wells.

We are not so sanguine. Unless we can find a rational basis for belief in personal integrity, person-respecting societies will have to make serious compromises. Writers like Giorgio Agamben maintain that societies around the globe have already turned decisively away from respect for persons. Replacing the person-respecting societies of the past, he observes, we have a continuous state of emergency in which citizens are reduced to what he calls "bare

---

[34] Peter Baehr (2000) *The Portable Hannah Arendt* (London: Penguin Books, 2000), p. 327.

life." If we are forced to sustain our social practices without belief in personal integrity, our sense is that we will suffer degradation in both our personal and social lives. We do not want to declare the mission to recover "person" accomplished until we have considered a few of the ways personal possibilities would be systematically diminished if we could no longer affirm that a life of moral integrity is within everyone's reach.

Chapter 6

Prospects for Personhood

We have seen how in ancient times humans came to identify persons narratively as individual characters of resolve, how those founding narratives built the possibility of moral integrity into their understanding of persons, how our understanding of *personhood* was shaped by that provenance, and how that narrative grasp of personal identity continues to underwrite inferences we draw in making moral and legal judgments. We have traced our Western notion of personal identity to a particular Story. But the details of that Story are beside the point for our current purposes; we are interested only in the formal truth conditions for a Story's character claims. As we are using the term, the 'Story' that underwrites moral integrity denotes *any* narrative that fulfills its promise to fully integrate its teller's life both individually and interpersonally. Because the philosophical expression of that belief is ethical monotheism, we can acknowledge that doctrine's formal claims as the foundation for belief in moral integrity.

Living in a secular age, people are likely to assume that if Storytelling is at the source of whatever residual belief we may have in moral integrity and Storytelling is not rational—"rational" in the sense that it is coherent and amenable to confirmation or disconfirmation on the basis of evidence—it is irrational to believe in moral integrity. Their alternative is to turn to causal explanations to account for human conduct. Against such skepticism we have argued that ethical monotheism (character logically understood) *can* be confirmed or refuted on the basis of evidence available in principle to everyone. In that fundamental sense, it qualifies as a rational doctrine.

This final chapter explains why we think person-respecting societies have a great deal riding on the issue of whether a life of moral integrity is possible. We will see that without that belief we are diminished in what we see as the scope of our active and interactive lives and in the historical significance of what we do. We will look both at negative consequences that follow from the absence of respect for moral integrity and at positive ways respect for moral integrity can enrich us as a person-respecting society.

How addressing someone by name would lose some of its power to call

Let's consider first what meaning we can hear in a person's name. We call people by name both to address them and to refer to them. "Jay, don't you dare tell Bea about Kay." "Please pass the peas, Dee." "Effie, what's a six letter word meaning 'intentional behavior?'" "Casey, don't strike out!" In this section, we are going to focus on the addressing function of personal names.

One thing we can say about these addresses is that they are all intended to provoke a certain active response. The action in response is intended to be characterized by the speaker's intent. To be called by name is to be invited to interact in a specified manner. "Listen to me, Jay! "The doctor will see you now, Kay." "Take a seat, Bea." "Hey, Dee, get off my lawn." Each initiates the sharing of an intention: to lend an attentive ear, take the seat, rise and follow, or flee never to return.

The examples in the last paragraph illustrate impersonal callings-by-name. They use somebody's personal name but do not issue an invitation to share a character of resolve. Theirs is only an invitation to share the character of some discrete action. So let us now turn to some examples that address somebody personally: "I, Bea, take thee, Jay, to be my wedded husband." "Jay, I want you to promise not to tell Bea about Kay." In these examples, it is the character of someone's resolve that is being engaged, and it is the sharing in the caller's resolve that is being called forth.

But among such personal addresses there are two ways to construe the appeal. If we do not believe that a life of moral integrity is possible for every person, we address a person in forensic contests as someone at best only relatively successful in the coordination of his intentional life and only relatively healthy in his interactions.

If, however, we do believe in the axiom of moral integrity then no matter how personally compromised the person we address may be, we address someone for whom a life of moral integrity is assumed to be possible. That means that in addition to calling him by his forensic name—a person with the normal rights and responsibilities we all bear—we call on him as the greater person he can be. We address him as someone who might, in response to our invitation, be drawn into a joint action that requires personal integrity and relational unity. That is the sense of "calling" Luther labeled "vocation."

It will seem to many that the notion of hearing one's name as a call to personal wholeness is anachronistic. In this, we freely acknowledge that they have a point. Long ago, people assumed a second name for their role in a Story of wholeness, as in Abram/Abraham, Simon/Peter, Saul/Paul, or the addition of Abdullah to a Muslim convert's given name. In that continuing tradition, when a Catholic celebrated his saint's day, being called by the saint's name invited him to celebrate his better self. But it has to be granted that though some of these patterns persist, their reverberations have largely faded in popular consciousness.

Even so, they are far from dying out. There continue to be occasions when people call someone by name as a solicitation to their better nature, to a degree of wholeness that they think is narratively possible for the addressee to accomplish. Often it is in the form of a demand: "Jay, look me in the eye and tell me you aren't having an affair."

"Look me in the eye" is a telling request. Whether literally or figuratively, when we look someone in the eye and demand he look us in the eye, we are addressing the wholeness of personal being we think is there to be solicited. We look for more than a person who may be dissembling and stumbling through our interaction; we attempt to elicit the transparency of her moral self. This intimate solicitation affirms a depth of interpersonal relationship that encourages speaking and hearing the truth. Does it matter whether our use of another's name can function as that kind of calling? We've spent the greater part of our discussion on judgments we make of people morally and legally. In those realms of discourse, we address one another to allow and disallow and to praise and blame. But we obviously cannot assume that all personal identifications are moral and legal. There are other realms in which we address someone aspiringly. When we encourage a child to do better in school, when we play the role of peacemaker, when we exchange vows, and when we forgive, we call the other to a self he can only have if a life of moral integrity is possible for him. The collapse of any rational basis for belief in that possibility, we fear, would hollow out the practices that best foster personhood.

How personal trust would be diminished

Our account has led us to represent the togetherness of two persons in the three temporal dimensions of their presence: in their immediate undertakings, in the future each projects, and in the past moments of resolve that contribute to the narrative context for their present resolve. Keeping in mind that thick temporality of interactive personal presence, consider how its volume might vary depending on whether we find it reasonable to assume the possibility of moral integrity.

Em's long-time friend Dee asks Em for a large unsecured loan to help her settle in a far-away country that has no extradition treaties. Em has known Dee long enough to feel confident in their friendship and in the sincerity of Dee's resolve to pay her back as soon as she finds her new footing.

If we imagine that Em believes that every person is capable of moral integrity, her confidence could run deep. She would be confident that Dee would never *have to* exploit her to aggrandize her own moment. She would never have to walk away from her agreement in order to live in good faith.

But now let us suppose that Em does *not* believe in moral integrity—perhaps the idea just doesn't make sense to her or perhaps she thinks it's just a wistful conceit. If that were the case, Em would have to allow for the possibility that Dee, someday, in order to pursue her greatest intentional satisfaction, will have to turn disloyal. If disloyalty held greater promise in terms of momentary satisfaction, Dee would have no personal choice but to be disloyal. It would not matter that she had been a faithful friend for years. Based on our current assumptions about Em's beliefs, she would have no strong reason to believe that Dee wouldn't have to betray her someday. If Dee shares Em's disbelief in moral integrity and came to find it personally expedient to renege on the loan, no personal obligation would stand in her way. If we assume that all moral obligations are personal obligations, Dee would no longer register her commitment to repay Em as morally obligatory. And of course Em could not in good conscience blame her for betraying her trust since she knows she would do the same thing if her own greatest intentional satisfaction depended on it.

Trust always involves going out on a limb. Em's act of trusting Dee would be risky even if both were believers. She knows that Dee might have a moral lapse in the future and fail to recognize where her best personal interests lie. But if Dee and Em believe in moral integrity, Em's confidence that Dee continues today as someone with personal responsibility for staying loyal would deepen Em's confidence in her and reinforce their friendship.

How the health of our social relations would be affected

We have illustrated how the quality of our personal relationships depends on whether we believe in moral integrity. Let us turn now to the question of how the axiom of moral integrity makes a difference in forensic reasoning in the broader realm of impersonal or social interactions. One clear challenge to our character logical account of personal rights, as we have presented it so far, is our intuitive regard for criminal conduct and its just dessert. Criminal activities exhibit the actor's resolution to accomplish his intentions at the expense of others. According to the axiom of moral integrity, the criminal is mistaken in the life he has chosen. But it is certainly not clear to criminals that virtue is its own reward. Indeed, their objective is typically to do the crime without doing the time. And when they are caught, tried, convicted, and sentenced, their desire to escape punishment is likely to be as strong as ever before. So we can assume a convict would, given the choice, opt out of his sentence if he were permitted to do so. He would prefer returning to the mean streets or executive suites where he could go on living a life resolved around exploiting others. The challenge this poses for our account is that, although we do not accept the convict's absolute right claim, the fact that we hold him personally responsible affirms his status as a person, thus as a rights holder. How then can we square depriving him of his freedom while still respecting him as a person?

To rise to this challenge, we need to take a closer look at the reasoning we use in criminal justice. We think we can demonstrate that character logic is complete (covering cases that seem at first to resist inclusion), internally consistent, and useful in suggesting how a correctional institution could be designed to be both fully person-respecting and optimally effective.

Much of the confusion about criminal rights can be blamed on the usual suspect, a faulty assumption about personal identity. When category logic and causal thinking gained the upper hand, a misunderstanding of personal identity emerged, one that did not distinguish adequately between persons and other beings. Humans were conceived as persisting beings rather than active momentary beings. We have seen in other forensic contexts how this misunderstanding systematically distorts our reasoning, and that is perniciously true in our thinking about crime and punishment.

There are two faulty accounts of identity that preclude treating convicts with respect. The first issues from Kant, which is ironic considering that he explicitly rejects causal explanations of human conduct and is normally regarded as an advocate of universal human respect. Though many of his ideas were revolutionary, he uncritically adopted an approach to forensic issues that is dependent on category logic. By Kant's account, the convict revealed the true nature of his persisting being when he broke the law. Since the convict can be assumed to have been free at the time he committed the crime, anything less than a level of punishment commensurate with the crime would fail to treat the lawbreaker with the respect he deserves as a free being. The convict revealed himself as a forensic character by the immoral rules he lived and presumably lives by. In this view, to treat him with personal respect is to treat him by the rules by which he has chosen to live.

Here we find a concrete application of Kant's categorical imperative. In the first of its three formulations, the imperative demands that we act only on the basis of a maxim that can be willed as universal law. Kant employed this formulation to show that actions such as murder, theft, and lying do not pass rational muster because they ultimately yield a self-contradiction. If we steal, for example, we implicitly affirm that everyone should steal. But if theft became the norm rather than the exception, it would undermine the institution of private property, which would, in a beautiful irony, preclude the possibility of theft. We are not concerned here with the merits of Kant's ethics except to say that his ideas on criminal justice apply that principle. In this case, the irrational endorsement of a maxim that cannot be universalized without offending against reason becomes, for Kant, a justification for treating convicts by the code of ethics their criminal conduct implicitly endorses. For our current purposes, the most significant upshot of Kant's theory is that it fixes the identity of the offender as the character of his *past* criminal act. This denies his status as the present character of his resolve, so by our account it is theoretically mistaken. It is also, as we will argue below, a serious practical mistake if correction is the goal.

The other confusion, though less sophisticated philosophically, betrays the same basic misunderstanding. It denies that criminals, as such, have any rights. People sometimes say things like, "He lost his rights when he committed the crime" or "Since he didn't recognize his victim's rights, he no longer has any claim on our recognition of his." This of course is also a mistake in that it fails to recognize the seat of personal rights in what it means to be a character of resolve.

What makes these misunderstandings of identity pernicious is that they both tend to work against what a person-respecting, person-fostering society should expect from its "correctional" institutions. We assume that the term "correction" in this context is intended to convey a social interest in bringing about a change in the convict, a change from one character to another. The first is a character in whom criminal action is integral, the second a character in whom criminal action would represent personal defeat. The Quakers in 18th century Philadelphia recognized this objective by calling their correctional institutions "penitentiaries," using this term to highlight the "change of heart" intrinsic to genuine correction.

The two assumptions about identity—that it persists through a lifetime and that a person can relinquish his rights—distort what "correction" should mean in the forensic context. To the extent they influence our penal system, they impede it.

A view of the convicted person as fixed in his identity as a character of criminal resolve means that any "change of heart" he may undergo in prison cannot change the fact that he is the same person he was when he committed the crime. That tends to mandate that the only basis for pronouncing him corrected is that he has served out his sentence. This assumption has two other untoward consequences. First, it stigmatizes the convict in the eyes of society at large. After being released, the ex-convict finds it difficult to reenter society. Second, the assumption cannot but make its way into the minds of the convicts themselves. Instead of embarking on a new path by resolving one's life anew, the convict resigns himself to being "who he is." Correctional institutions, instead of facilitating the sort of transformation that would equip convicts to reenter and contribute to society, become training centers where convicts learn how to avoid getting caught in the next go-around. Having entered prison as criminals, convicts all too often emerge from prison as hardened criminals.

The other pernicious assumption—that criminals have relinquished their personal rights—also tends to work against genuinely corrective treatment. If the criminal has no personal rights, the only constraint on the severity of his punishment becomes the severity of his crime. This allows for and frequently leads to the destruction of inmates. By tacitly condoning violence, prison officials make it virtually imperative for inmates to form protective alliances. The result is that prisons are hotbeds of gang formation. This clearly violates the spirit that would be present in a genuinely correctional institution since gang-centered lives are resolved around unhealthy interactions.

For as far back in history as we have respected persons socially as bearing intrinsic rights and responsibilities, we have done so by proscribing practices that de-personalize. The American founding fathers (following the English Bill of Rights) marked depersonalizing treatment as "cruel and unusual." One thing 18th-century corporal punishments have in common with 21st century incarceration is that their cruelty is not simply that they make a convict miserable but that they systematically destroy him as a person by precluding his capacity to live a life of healthy resolve.

What seems to have distorted our reasoning on this issue is the modern tendency to treat the person as a locus of experience. If the threshold of "cruel and unusual" punishment is experiential, it gets measured by the level of intensity of the pain we are justified in inflicting. It is of course true that pain can destroy a person[35] and when it is experienced in repeated episodes it is likely to debilitate the subject's active capacities for the future. But if we allow ourselves to use pain-thresholds as our criterion for what counts as "cruel and unusual," we give ourselves license to overlook person-destroying punishments that do not involve pain. The most egregious of these is solitary confinement, particularly for long stretches of time. That kind of confinement prevents an inmate from leading an inwardly complex life, denies him interactivity, and prevents him from doing anything of historical importance. By

---

[35] Elaine Scarry, in *The Body in Pain: The Making and Unmaking of the World* (Oxford University Press, 1985), argues that imposing acute pain destroys the subject's world. Since human agents can only act in a world, this amounts to destroying them personally.

blocking all three dimensions of personal self-actualization, solitary confinement destroys not only the convict's personal story as a criminal but his capacity to tell a personal story at all. Needless to say, this precludes correction.

So, the first rule of "correction" in a person-respecting society is that it must not destroy the capacity to be a corrected person. That, however, raises the question of what person-respecting punishment is supposed to do. Unless we answer that question, we invite ourselves to think of punishment as an end in itself. But if correction is the end, punishment must be understood as a means. Specifically, the point of punishing someone must be to move him to correct himself, to move him to shift his identity in the forensically relevant way.

One way to see more clearly how punishment works correctionally is to represent it in conjunction with rehabilitation. Although punishment and rehabilitation are often thought of as the twin goals of "correction," it is universally recognized that there is a tension between them and that accommodating both is difficult. Character logic locates the tension in the effects on agency the two phases of treatment represent. Punishment is designed to take moment away from the convict while rehabilitation is meant to enliven patterns of his interactive health, which (when successful) has the effect of augmenting his moment. The borderland can be negotiated in a principled way if we take into account the shift in forensic identity correction is intended to achieve. If someone who has been identified as a character of criminal resolve comes to present himself as a character of non-criminal resolve (the correctional institution having done its job), the punishment he suffered can be seen as having been directed at one forensic person and the rehabilitation directed at (fostering) another. This has important implications in practice. If punishment is directed only at the character of criminal resolve, it ought not to go beyond undoing that specific character. If it does go beyond that objective and debilitates the capacity for healthy resolve or dismantles the person altogether, it impedes healthy interactions, thus preventing rehabilitation from achieving its corrective purpose.

As corrective treatment begins, the initial assumption, almost always born out, is that the person entering the system is the same person who committed the crime. By our account, that means his present resolve is narratively coherent with his story at the time he committed the crime. He presents initially as a continuation of that character.

The initial objective of institutional correction is to disrupt that continuity. To that end, it will have to do two things: make it impossible for him to continue in his criminal character of resolve and make it possible for him to tell a new story. People rarely make radical shifts in their lives, and they never do so without good reason. That is why we are generally justified in assuming that we each bear continuing character from one meeting to another. We know that the only good reason for becoming discontinuous with one's former character of resolve is that the old way of life no longer works. The first step in corrective treatment, therefore, should be to prevent the convict from putting his life together in the same unhealthy way. Society is obliged to arrest him, detain him, hold him, confine him as a person, all for the purpose of deactivating the character of resolve he has been and continues to be at that time.

As we saw earlier, what keeps this from being a denial of his personal right to absolve is the belief that he can—if he resolves to—lead a life of healthy interactions to his greater self-actualization. His basis for claiming an absolute right (vis a vis the judicial system) is based in the claim that he can actualize himself most fully by exploiting others. For believers in moral integrity, that is an irrational claim and cannot be honored.

Our argument here is akin in function to J. S. Mill's for setting limits to another's right to self-determination. As a rule, we defer to an individual's choice since we presume him to be in the best position to judge what will give him the most satisfaction. If someone thinks he will diminish his personal prospects unless he gets away for a vacation, opens a tanning salon, takes up bungee jumping, or drops his Netflix account, we accord him the right to do so (assuming he does so rightfully) even when we are of the opinion that he's making a mistake.

But suppose we were to find someone doing something that wasn't just *improbable* as a path to his greatest accomplishment but absolutely *inconceivable* as one. In that case, we would feel justified in trying to prevent him, for example, from driving home drunk, yielding to opioids, or, to cite Mill's example, selling himself into slavery. If we believe in moral integrity, we are justified by the possibilities we find in personal stories in denying the convict the right to absolve from his sentence. In denying his claim, we would not be joining those who believe convicts give up their rights when they commit crimes. Nor would we be joining those who claim that criminals, when they commit their crimes, relinquish their personhood. Instead, we would be denying his claim to absolve because of our conviction that it would be impossible for him (or anyone) to achieve his greatest personal good by living exploitatively. By trying to correct him we are leading him in accord with his best interests, even if he cannot see that now.

So, the motion to absolve on personal grounds is denied. Now the correctional regimen commences. But how? What kind of treatment do we expect at the beginning of the convict's term at the correctional institution? Society answers this question most emphatically in terms of punishment. We, the members of a person-respecting society, expect our correctional institutions to punish offenders. It is right that they be punished.

There are those who regard the urge to punish as an atavistic impulse to be tamed or another of those pre-scientific ideas culturally embedded by the peculiarities of our traditions. This line of thought began in earnest in the eighteenth century, when Cesare Beccaria argued that most punishments are retaliatory and vengeful. He proposed a more scientific alternative based on utilitarian principles. By promoting deterrence, he hoped his alternative would maximize society's overall happiness. In the twentieth century the view was best represented by the psychiatrist Karl Menninger.[36]

But that is not where our account leads us. Society's felt need to punish has character logical as well as cultural roots. Our intuitive sense that wrongdoers deserve punishment need not be explained as an impulse from our reptilian brain or the prompting of a violent heritage. It can also be explained by the paradigm we use in identifying persons. And that is why it matters which paradigm we adopt. If we look at a convict and see both the presence of a character resolved around criminal action and the possibility of a character resolved more successfully around non-criminal activity, we can put punishment into functional focus as the prompt required for the convict's movement from one character identity to the other.

How are we supposed to imagine this happening? There is some insight, we think, in considering three common reasons people give to justify punishment. Though each has an intuitive basis, that basis gets systematically distorted when we reason with mistaken ideas about identity. People insist, first, that a convict owes a *debt* to society, second, that he deserves to *suffer* for his crime, and, third, that his punishment is needed to express society's *condemnation* of the act and the actor. Seeing how the distortion sabotages our understanding of these three justifications can help us to fit punishment more rationally into the process of correction.

"Paying one's debt to society" is intuitively grounded in the requirement that damage claims must be settled for someone's absolution to be justified. It trades on our recognition that a law-breaker (by definition) has deviated from some legally mandated social understanding and thereby caused someone harm. His rightful absolution requires him to compensate for the loss of moment he caused.

Yet, while paying one's debt to society does have a role in correction, that role gives it no lines until the final act. It does not play reasonably in the first act, the punitive stage of correction, because thinking of punishment as pay-

---

[36]Menninger, Karl *The Crime of Punishment.* NY: Penguin Books, 1968

back equates the status of being corrected with the status of having paid one's debt to society. Since the latter has been determined by the length of the sentence, punishment is mandated to be carried out even past the time of the convict's correction. By then, punishment has lost its point and becomes only an impediment to rehabilitation.

"Paying one's debt" is dangerous when used as a justification for punishment because the demand it represents, when meted out in years behind bars, undermines the achievement of correction. Its intuitive force will need to be discussed at the end of the process of correction when the treatment of the convicted person again becomes civil.

The second rationale people use to justify punishment is that people who take advantage of others deserve to suffer. This is another of those elements of folk psychology widely thought to defy rational justification, which is why people who cite this justification for punishment are sometimes thought to be giving in to a vengeful impulse or a puritan proclivity. To appreciate the rational force of the demand for suffering, we have to suspend our modern tendency to think of suffering as an experience and return to thinking of it as a quality of a person's active awareness.

As we mentioned before, the scientific era has accustomed us to think of suffering in terms of experience. As we also noted, a bit of etymology can peel back the experiential kind of suffering to reveal the kind we are actively aware of. Before the modern era, "suffering" meant "letting happen," as when King James' Jesus asks his listeners to "suffer the little children…to come unto me." "Suffering" in this relevant forensic sense is simply the opposite of "acting." That a convict deserves to suffer does not necessarily mean that he deserves to have pain imposed on him. Instead, from the perspective of character logic, it means that he deserves to have imposed on him the inaction required to deactivate his exploitative resolve. Think of how people suffer during a hospital stay. Some will suffer pain and discomfort; all will suffer deactivation. Their "stay" constitutes a "confinement" that imposes a hiatus on their projects. They are bidden to be a "patient" instead of an agent.

It is this older sense of suffering as the deactivation of someone's character of resolve that justifies punishment. It may entail a certain amount of physical discomfort for most people, to be sure, but suffering experientially is not the point. Incarceration suffers the convict to rebuild resolve around healthy relationships.

The challenge for correctional institutions is to draw limits to experiential suffering so that it does not impede the emergence of a new character of resolve. Early in our culture's attempts to be person-respecting, judges drew that line at punishments deemed "cruel and unusual." Justice William Brennan gave it an operational reading in 1972 when he maintained "that a punishment must not by its severity be degrading to human dignity."[37] We believe we can survey the boundary proposed by Brennen with greater precision if we say that punishment must not by its severity undermine somebody's ability and right to become an interactively healthy person. It is enough for society to deconstruct criminal resolve; it is counterproductive to do so by impeding or precluding the convict's projection of a healthy life.

The third rationale people sometimes cite for punishment is that it is the only way society can express its condemnation of the criminal and his crime. As a society we need to affirm our shared sense of the rightful boundaries of our interactions. Punishment alone seems reprobative enough to keep those lines indelible.

The word "condemnation" feels vaguely inappropriate in a secular era. It conjures up Dantean nightmares and Cotton Mather's sermons. But it's apparent that these hoary tropes, so convincing to our ancestors, were predicated on the assumption that persons were, metaphysically speaking, entities. An entity is identifiably what it is for as long as it exists. Persons, being eternal entities, were thus understood to persist as culpable beings forever, therefore justly punished forever.

So, let us rethink condemnation in terms of the distinctive temporal logic we use when we reason about characters of resolve. Condemnation in the old conceptual framework represents complete personal annihilation. Personal annihilation means the annihilation of someone's active moment to the point that he cannot sustain his current character of resolve. In that sense, "condemnation" perfectly expresses society's reprobation. It is an absolute NO to an act and its actor. But as long as there are new, more momentous possibilities for personal resolve available, this depletion of moment is meant to be temporary. Its function is to open up space for the condemned to learn to self-actualize in a new interactive context. This needs to be emphasized: condemnation is only appropriate to society's interests when it is accompanied by the provision of healthy interactive alternatives. Only then can we see societal condemnation as instrumental to the convict's coming to actualize a character healthy enough to stay within the law.

The key to balancing punishment and rehabilitation is to appreciate that the two modes of treatment are directed to different forensic persons—one to the character of criminal resolve, the other to the character of non-criminal resolve. At the beginning of the convict's sentence, the two modes run concurrently. After correction takes place, when the convict is genuinely trying to

---

[37] Furman v. Georgia, 408 U.S. 238

sustain interactive health but has yet to stabilize himself in a new story, punishment must loosen its hold. In this stage of the correctional process, the inmate ought to be encouraged to initiate new relationships, learn vocational skills, and practice the coping skills he'll need to negotiate what he is likely to encounter following his release.

This may sound like a utopian demand. To foster relational health among a population continually degraded by an influx of interactively unhealthy people would be challenging even if unlimited resources were available. But it is a challenge that must be accepted if we are to preserve our status as a person-respecting society. It may be merely tautologous (character logically) to say that only health can beget health, but that formal truth inscribes a mandate on prisons to be respectful environments so that the correctional process has a legitimate chance of doing its job.

The other institutional challenge in making treatment respectful arises when a judgment must be made whether a convict's correction is a *fait accompli*, or at least underway. When should we accredit the promise of sustaining non-criminal resolve? What makes this determination so challenging is that the only people who can reasonably judge whether someone has begun to tell a new personal story are people who know him personally. That makes discerning his status problematic for an institution. But it would be a mistake to let such practical concerns obscure the fact that whether or not someone has undergone a corrective change is an actual fact about him. We must acknowledge that there is (in principle) a basis for judging whether he has begun to establish a healthy life and whether he has stabilized with enough ballast to tell his (forensically) new story in good faith.

Finally, there is a step in the correctional process that is rarely taken but is known to be of assistance following a person's release from incarceration. For correction to find its footing, the inmate's status as "corrected" must be affirmed by society. If we assume that personal health can only come with interactive health, correction is finally achieved only with the released convict's reintegration into the society he once wronged, sometimes even into the personal relationships he offended. He will have to address us (our shared society) in a new way, and we him.

Criminologist John Braithwaite characterizes this occasion of re-engagement as an act of "reintegrative shaming."[38] Braithwaite's term makes sense when we imagine the passage as a kind of forensic graduation ceremony from one personal identity to another and, accordingly, from one social

---

[38] Braithwaite, John (1989). *Crime, Shame, and Reintegration.* Cambridge: Cambridge University Press.

status to another. The convict's change of heart requires his present shame because his past character, as an offender, now registers with negative personal value (its actualization having subtracted past moments from his new personal presence by voiding much of his history). Acknowledging shame means repudiating those moments of offensive action by testifying to their present negative polarity. It means proclaiming that, were he to incorporate them into his story now, they would dissolve him. He has to be ashamed of who he was in order to say who he is. He must show us how the depletion his past visits upon his presence shrinks him and makes him cower. The word "shame" is thought to derive from the gesture of covering oneself, Adam's gesture when God came walking through the garden. When for the sake of his new integration a person forswears an offensive part of his past, his presence must cover that past with a fig leaf of self-reproach.

"Reintegrative shaming" as a template for rejoining society also represents an interactive achievement, not something a corrected person can do by himself. In the shaming, he addresses the society he offended, identifies himself as a shamed person and as a person who asks to be accepted into the cooperative arrangement he once abused. For his bid to be successful, society has to accept it. Forensically, that means welcoming him back into society by restoring his full share of civic rights, like the right to vote and eligibility for public employment and benefits.

Reintegrative shaming is analogous to the reconciliation often enacted after an interpersonal rupture: the absolver says he is sorry and the offended person forgives him; the ex-con says he is ashamed and society welcomes him back as a respected member. But if that analogy is to hold, presumably the ex-con has to try to "make it up" to those he offended.

When we discussed the analogy between punishment and payment of debt—an analogy used to justify punishment—we acknowledged that the payment of damages required in civil cases does indeed apply in criminal cases. By breaking the law, as Socrates argued, the criminal damages society. At the same time, we objected to the thesis that *punishment* is the payback. We objected because such thinking distorts our decisions about how correction should proceed. It invites us to think of correction as having been achieved only when the time has been served instead of when the shift in forensic identity is either significantly underway or completed. That observation led us to separate the punitive obligation from the debt-paying obligation and to defer the latter to the end of the process. Only in the final step, when the reintegrated person resumes his role in society, should that obligation be negotiated and discharged.

Now that he is back in the civil realm, one might assume that the newly reentered person is obliged to pay for the damage he did. But it's more complicated than that. For one thing, the amount of damage his crime did may well be beyond what can be repaid. If you fail to shovel the snow from your sidewalk and someone slips and breaks an ankle, you are liable for your breach of social responsibility—your absolution from its rules—and obligated to pay for the damages accordingly. One would hope you could pay for what you caused without any threat to your personhood. But it is important to recognize that your obligation is limited to what you can personally afford. The sustaining of your personal resolve takes precedence over the payment of the debt. Thus, people who declare bankruptcy are never forced into personal insolvency. The court will set them back but not wipe them out. The same person-respecting principle applies to the former convict. Though society can justifiably exact a payback, it cannot justifiably undermine the person he newly is.

Moreover, since the ex-convict is a fledgling in the character of his non-criminal resolve, the burden of reparations he could take on without being crushed is likely to be relatively light. Since society's greater interest is in the former convict's personal success and since jeopardizing that success would be damaging for both the former convict and society, he has a personal right to a manageable debt burden. In the end, then, "paying one's debt to society," while it reasonably engages the logic of rightful absolution, has little cash value in the re-integrative process.

This survey of the stages of correction demonstrates how, by assuming the possibility of moral integrity, we can justify punishment while also maximizing the chances for rehabilitation. When we include the axiom of moral integrity in our character logic, penal practices that are person-respecting turn out to be optimally corrective. They illustrate how belief in moral integrity enhances the health of our interactive life by preserving and extending the community of mutual social respect.

Diminishing the historical importance of what we do

Having seen some of the ways the momentary value of our active and interactive lives is systematically enhanced when we operate with the axiom of moral integrity, we now turn to the question of how that axiom allows us to understand the ongoing importance of what we do. You will recall that we distinguished an act's critical historical importance from its actual historical importance, critical importance being reckoned in terms of effects and actual importance in terms of the momentary weight of the accomplishment intended. Archduke Ferdinand's assassination was critically important in that it proved the catalyst for World War I. It was actually important to the young

Serb for what he (reportedly) meant to do: strike a blow for southern Slavic independence. Since an intended action's movement over time is one of the factors determining the volume of its active presence, a person who sees himself advancing long-term accomplishments, especially accomplishments that extend beyond his lifespan, not only sees importance in what he is doing but actualizes himself as a more momentous person in resolving to actualize those extended historical accomplishments. The opposite is just as apparent. If someone busies himself exclusively with quotidian tasks, he would not feel particularly edified by them. If those tasks defined how he made his living, it would be "just a job."

In light of our awareness of the extended importance our actions can have, it is sobering to consider how the cultural and technological arenas for social agency now militate against it. Using electronic technologies, for example, seems to pull our imagination into ever foreshortened projections of achievement, even to the point of being virtually durationless (like an Internet search or a Wall Street trade). And as our imaginative projections tend to be more occupied with short-term projects, longer-term projects may get less attention than they need to sustain their coordination. Academicians find students less prepared to put the term into a term paper, corporation managers and shareholders find themselves focusing on short-term results to the detriment of long-term value, and governments put off infrastructure maintenance and timely responses to environmental concerns. Movies are, more often than not, fast-paced action thrillers, marriages more often serial, jobs more often temporary, and investments more often short term.

One of the ways people manifest their awareness of the threat this temporal foreshortening poses is by fetishizing an ultimacy of moment for one of the other dimensions of their active being. Some try to compensate for diminished historical moment by aiming for a perfectly integrated inner life (through meditation, for instance). Some aim for a romantic relationship that could so occupy their intentional life that each partner would find perfect resolution living in the orb of their togetherness.

But because the richest personal life is significant in all three of its dimensions of active moment, there is no adequate compensation for the diminished historical moment. Just as a historical footing is required to give stability to identity, the projection of a future history is integral to a sense of personal well-being. It is difficult, therefore, to see diminished historical importance as anything but diminished personal being. While both meditation and deep interpersonal attachment may promise and (for many) deliver some enhancement of momentary awareness, neither can fully compensate a person for his loss of ongoing importance.

Here again, belief in moral integrity makes an important difference. It provides a bulwark against foreshortening active awareness to the point of undermining personal integrity. Since a morally integral life advances some course of action that bears the form of a Story, its teller enjoys the confidence that in her moments of action and interaction, whatever the scope of their immediate achievement, she is building a community of personal respect and personal support that advances what is ultimately momentous.

The Promise of Sustained Personhood

Finally, what can we conclude about the prospects for personhood? In this chapter we have argued that these prospects are enhanced if we find grounds for believing in personal integrity. It is the height of folly to allow a doctrine about the contingency of meaning to lead us to deconstruct persons into aleatory tumbles of signifiers, as though momentary being could only be elusive, fictive, multi-phrenic, protean, saturated, fractured, and ephemeral. It is folly because it does not do justice to the resolution we achieve in building our relational lives around ongoing projects. No matter how much foreshortening there may be in the courses of movement we project, we can depend on our nature as multi-intentioned agents to continue to project action into the future.

So, there is a limit to how much historical significance we can expect to lose. As long as we exist as multi-intentioned agents, we will continue to be creatures who tell a personal story. Since maximizing moment is our innate vocation and not some challenge imposed on us contingently by the conditions of our development, we will always carve out self-referential narrative identity. Our successors, like us, will be planted in a history, their own and that of their interactive communities, planted in moments whose historical significance their character of resolve will determine as most important to them.

Yet this character logical assurance should not make us entirely sanguine about the prospects for personhood. We have seen that the protocols of personal respect depend on a robust sense of moving an accomplishment that transcends our life-spans. Without being resolved around historically significant achievements, one is tempted to become feckless and inconstant. Can we dare to hope that the ways in which we identify and foster persons will maintain their regency over moral and legal reasoning even if persons have little momentary reach beyond their daily routines? If you are as uncertain as we are when faced with that question, the vision of being builders of future moment through lives of moral integrity can stand as our final illustration of the sort of difference that axiom makes.

We live in times when the ancient Stories have largely been commandeered by people who cannot tell them authentically and who use them exploitatively. We live in times when intellectual traditions give category reasoning supremacy in ways that ignore the personal identifications we make in everyday interactions. To at least some extent, that cannot but tend to undermine our confidence that belief in moral integrity will continue to inform our judgments.

Yet, even if we have become too proud or too sophisticated to tell a Story, perhaps we can still find reason to hope that there is a Story to be told. Perhaps we can still aspire to live in confidence that there is personal worth in a life of moral integrity. We end then on a tentative but hopeful note. We have seen that "person" can indicate an actual individual being about whom we can make reasonable moral and legal judgments. We have found that its significant form, that of a personal story, discloses the kind of personal identification that governs forensic reasoning and defines the being of a person as historical.

We have also seen that our practice of identifying persons as individual characters of resolve retains certain features of the logic of its origin, features that make it reasonable to underwrite the assumptions we make about moral integrity. Whether the evidence supports the formal possibility of Storytelling will determine how we think of personhood's prospects. Deciding whether hope in moral integrity is justified by the evidence will shape how we can address one another personally, how inclusively we can sustain our communities of mutual respect, and how momentously we can aspire to accomplishments that transcend us.

The Axioms of Character Logic

These axioms reflect formal features of character claims ('A did C' claims) and, except for the last axiom, their entailments.

The axiom of active being: any act we characterize has its being in the moves that accomplish it. Since every move represents a moment of movement, an act's temporal being comprises its moments of movement and registers with greater or lesser moment according to their sum.

The axiom of agent identity: to identify any agent is to determine the range of action properly ascribable to him.

The axiom of resolve: a person's action is resolved when he projects his future course of accomplishment to accommodate the satisfaction of a number of his present intentions.

The axiom of personal resolve: a person's action is personally resolved when someone projects it to best satisfy his intentional life as a whole.

The axiom of self-actualization: a person is resolved to actualize himself in all three dimensions of his personal agency—in his individual life, in his interactive life, and in the historical movement he advances.

The axiom of good faith: a person enjoys good faith when his practical imagination warrants confidence that the personal resolve he projects will actualize him most momentously.

The axiom of interactive presence: a person is present with another when they are in the same active moment, and they are in the same active moment when they are moving the same character of accomplishment.

The axiom of personal presence: a person is present with another personally when each projects his interactive role not only to accomplish his own good faith requirements but those of the other as well.

The axiom of interactive health: a person enjoys a healthy interaction with another person when both parties are acting in good faith.

The axiom of personal rights: a person has the positive right to pursue interactions that promise to actualize him most and the absolute right to absolve from any interaction or any offer to interact if it precludes that optimal being, but only if he compensates the other party for any moment he loses thereby.

The axiom of personal responsibility: a person is personally responsible for all and only the actions determined in character by his present resolve. That makes him responsible for all that he is presently doing resolutely, for projecting the most promising future course he can imagine and for those past moments of resolve he can tell as earlier episodes of his present story.

The axiom of personal integrity: a person enjoys personal integrity when the whole of her intentional life is comprehended in her resolve.

The axiom of moral integrity: a person can achieve integrity, but only in healthy interactions. This axiom does not follow from the others. What evidence if any we have for it is the topic of chapter 5.

Bibliography

Agamben, Giorgio (2005) *State of Exception*, Kevin Attell, trans, Chicago: University of Chicago Press.

Arendt, Hannah (1978) *The Life of the Mind: Thinking*. New York: Harcourt, Brace, Jovanovich.

Aristotle *Nicomachean Ethics* Book III, Ch. 5 in McKeon.

Baehr, Peter (2000) *The Portable Hannah Arendt*. London: Penguin Books.

Baker, Lynne Rudder (2000) *Persons and Bodies: A Constitution View*. Cambridge University Press.

Beauvoir, Simone de (2009) *The Second Sex*, Constance Borde and Sheila Malovany-Chevallier, trans., London: Jonathan Cape.

Beccaria, Cesare (2003) *On Crimes and Punishments and Other Writings*, Richard Davies, trans., Cambridge University Press.

Boethius (1998) "A Treatise Against Eutyches and Nestorius," *The Theological Treatises*, translated by H. F. Stewart London: Heinemann.

Braithwaite, John (1989). *Crime, Shame, and Reintegration*. Cambridge: Cambridge University Press.

Derrida, Jacques (1976) *Of Grammatology*, Gayatri Chakravorty Spivak, trans. Baltimore: Johns Hopkins University Press.

Derrida, Jacques (1978) *Writing and Difference*, Alan Bass, trans., Chicago: University of Chicago Press.

Davidson, Donald (1980) *Essays on Actions and Events*. Oxford: Oxford University Press.

Duberman, Martin (1991) *Cures: a Gay Man's Odyssey*. New York: Dutton.

Fletcher, George (1978) *Rethinking Criminal Law*. Boston: Little Brown and Company.

Fried, Charles (1981) *Contract as Promise*. Cambridge, Massachusetts and London, England: Harvard University Press.

Gilligan, Carol "Hearing the Difference: Theorizing Connection," Hypatia, vol. 10, no. 2 (Spring 1995).

Gombrich, E. H. (2000) *Art and Illusion* Princeton and Oxford: Princeton University Press Bollingen Series XXXV.

Griswold, Charles L. (2007) *Forgiveness: A Philosophical Exploration*. Cambridge: Cambridge University Press.

Hoekema, David A. "African Personhood: Morality and Identity in the 'Bush of Ghosts'," *Soundings* 91.3-4 (Fall/Winter 2008).

Hume, David (1739/1978) *A Treatise of Human Nature*. 2nd ed. Ed. L.A. Selby-Bigge, text rev. P. H. Nidditch. Oxford: Clarendon Press.

Hohfeld, Wesley Newcomb (1919) *Fundamental Legal Conceptions*. New Haven: Yale University Press.

James, Gene G. "The Orthodox Theory of Civil Disobedience," *Social Theory and Practice*, Vol. 2. No. 4 (Fall 1973).

James, William (1981) *The Varieties of Religious Experience* New York: Penguin Books.

Lacan, Jacques (2006) *Écrits*, Bruce Fink, trans., New York: Norton.

Locke, John (1961) *Essay Concerning Human Understanding*. London: J. M. Dent and NY: Dutton.

Lyotard, Jean-François (1984) *The Postmodern Condition: A Report on Knowledge*, Geoff Bennington and Brian Massumi, trans. Manchester: Manchester University Press.

McFall, Lynne (1987) "Integrity," *Ethics* 98.

McKeon, Richard, ed. (1941) *The Basic Works of Aristotle*. New York: Random House

Menninger, Karl (1968) *The Crime of Punishment.* NY: Penguin Books

Nussbaum, Martha C. (2016) *Anger and Forgiveness: Resentment, Generosity, Justice* New York: Oxford University Press.

Parfit, Derek (1984) *Reasons and Persons.* Oxford: Clarendon Press

Prust, Richard C. (2004) *Wholeness: the Character Logic of Christian Belief.* Amsterdam and New York: Rodopi Press.

Scarry, Elaine (1985) *The Body in Pain: The Making and Unmaking of the World* Oxford and New York: Oxford University Press.

Strawson, Galen (2004) "Against Narrativity" in *Ratio (new series)* XVII 4 December 2004, p. 432.

Strawson, Peter (1959) *Individuals* (London: Methuen).

Suchon, Gabrielle (2010) *On the Celibate Life Freely Chosen, or Life Without Commitments* in Gabrielle Suchon, *A Woman Who Defends All the Persons of Her Sex: Selected Philosophical and Moral Writings*, Domna C. Stanton and Rebecca M. Wilkin, trans., The University of Chicago Press, 237-93.

Suchon, Gabrielle (2010) *Treatise on Ethics and Politics, Divided into three Parts: Freedom, Knowledge, and Authority* in Gabrielle Suchon, *A Woman Who Defends All the Persons of Her Sex: Selected Philosophical and Moral Writings*, Domna C. Stanton and Rebecca M. Wilkin, trans., The University of Chicago Press, 2010, 72-228.

Sverdlik, Steven (1993) "Pure Negligence" *American Philosophical Quarterly* 30 (2)

Swinburne, R. (1986) *The Evolution of the Soul.* Oxford: Clarendon Press.

Taylor, Gabriele (1981) "Integrity," *Proceedings of the Aristotelian Society Supplement* 55.

Taylor, Richard (1974) *Metaphysics*, 4th edition. Upper Saddle River, NJ: Prentice-Hall.

Teichman, Jenny (1985) "The Definition of a Person," *Philosophy* LX

Wakefield, Dan (1992) *New York in the Fifties.* NY: St. Martin's Press.

Index

A

Action, v, vi, vii, viii, ix, x, xi, xii, xiv,
2, 3, 4, 5, 6, 7, 8, 9, 10, 11, 12, 13,
14, 15, 17, 18, 19, 20, 21, 22, 23,
25, 26, 27, 28, 29, 30, 31, 32, 33,
39, 41, 46, 48, 50, 51, 57, 58, 59,
62, 63, 64, 65, 67, 68, 69, 71, 72,
73, 74, 75, 78, 79, 80, 81, 83, 84,
85, 86, 88, 89, 94, 97. 98, 102,
106, 108, 109, 111, 112
    Logic of action, xi
    Moment of action, xi, xiv, 62
Agamben, Giorgio, 90
Arendt, Hannah, 61, 66, 90
Aristotle, vii, 2, 63

B

Baehr, Peter, 90
Baker, Lynne Rudder, 1
Beauvoir, Simone de, 53
Beccaria, Cesare, 102
Boethius, 1
Braithwaite, John, 105

C

Category logic, vii, viii, ix, xii, xiv,
1, 2, 3, 25, 27, 41, 42, 65, 97
Character claims, vii, viii, ix, x, xiii,
2, 3, 4, 5, 8, 14, 19, 35, 39, 62, 78,
82, 93, 111
    Character claims that identify
    persons, v, xii
Character logic, vii, ix, x, xi, xiv, 2,
25, 26, 27, 33, 41, 42, 53, 54, 55,
58, 62, 70, 75, 76, 82, 97, 100,
103, 107, 111, 112
Character of resolve, vi, vii, x, xi,
xii, xiii, 2, 6, 8, 14, 15, 18, 20, 21,
24, 25, 26, 28, 31, 33, 35, 36, 38,
45, 48, 52, 53, 55, 57, 58, 59, 68,
69, 70, 71, 72, 73, 75, 83, 84, 88,
93, 94, 98, 100, 101, 103, 104,
109, 110
Civil disobedience, xii, 46, 47, 59

D

Davidson, Donald, 3
Derrida, Jacques, 2
Duberman, Martin, 80

F

Fletcher, George, 58
Fried, Charles, 45

G

Gilligan, Carol, 27
Gombrich, E. H., 78
Griswold, Charles L., 65

H

Hoekema, David A., 25
Hume, David, 2, 18

J

James, Gene G., 47

James, William, 60

L

Lacan, Jacques, 2
Legal rights and responsibilities, vi
Locke, John, 1, 18
Lyotard, Jean-François, 2

M

McFall, Lynne, 71
Menninger, Karl, 102
Monotheism, xiii, 72, 73, 76
    Ethical monotheism, xiii, 83, 84, 86, 87, 88, 89, 93
Moral integrity, xiii, xiv, 37, 47, 70, 71, 72, 75, 76, 81, 82, 83, 86, 87, 88, 90, 91, 93, 94, 95, 96, 101, 107, 109, 110, 112

N

Nussbaum, Martha C., 65, 66

P

Parfit, Derek, 19
Personal identity, v, vi, viii, ix, x, 1, 2, 7, 13, 14, 33, 65, 69, 71, 75, 93, 97, 105
Personal integrity, 6, 69, 70, 71, 72, 75, 76, 82, 90, 91, 94, 109, 112
Personal presence, x, xi, xii, 15, 17, 18, 19, 20, 25, 27, 33, 38, 59, 95, 106, 111
Personal resolve, x, xi, 7, 8, 9, 10, 12, 13, 14, 21, 26, 40, 42, 63, 67, 72, 75, 76, 82, 83, 104, 107, 111

Personal responsibility, v, vi, xii, 6, 17, 33, 57, 58, 59, 61, 62, 64, 67, 68, 96, 112
Personal rights, vii, x, xi, 17, 25, 33, 35, 37, 38, 40, 47, 51, 57, 70, 96, 98, 99, 101, 107, 112
Personal stories, x, xii, 1, 9, 10, 13, 14, 15, 16, 17, 23, 24, 25, 59, 67, 69, 71, 72, 77, 79, 80, 81, 82, 84, 89, 100, 101, 105, 109, 110
Person-fostering society, 17, 24, 43, 52, 53, 70, 90, 98
Person-respecting society, xiii, xiv, 17, 24, 35, 46, 52, 53, 70, 76, 89, 90, 93, 97, 98, 100, 102, 103, 107
Prust, Richard C., 26, 80

R

Resolve, vi, vii, x, xi, xiv, 3, 7, 8, 9, 10, 11, 12, 13, 14, 16, 17, 18, 19, 20, 26, 27, 28, 29, 30, 31, 36, 38, 40, 41, 42, 45, 46, 47, 48, 49, 50, 51, 53, 57, 59, 60, 61, 62, 63, 64, 66, 67, 69, 72, 73, 74, 75, 76, 79, 80, 84, 85, 87, 88, 94, 95, 98, 99, 100, 102, 103, 104, 105, 107, 111, 112
    Persons as characters of resolve, xi
    Present character of resolve, vi, xi, 6, 15, 19, 33, 35, 57, 69, 98

S

Scarry, Elaine, 99
Strawson, Galen, 15
Strawson, Peter, 1
Suchon, Gabrielle, 53
Sverdlik, Steven, 63

Swinburne, R., 4

T

Taylor, Gabriele, 71
Taylor, Richard, 11, 12
Teichman, Jenny, 1

W

Wakefield, Dan, 85

www.ingramcontent.com/pod-product-compliance
Lightning Source LLC
Chambersburg PA
CBHW050558300426
44112CB00013B/1980